# Cosmic Body
# Astrology

A Beginner's Guide to Using the Stars to Understand Yourself, Your Signs and Birth Chart, Use the Power of the Planets for Health, Healing, and Everyday Life

# Melissa Gomes

https://smartpa.ge/MelissaGomes

# Table of Contents

# FREEBIES

## AND

## RELATED PRODUCTS

**WORKBOOKS**
**AUDIOBOOKS**
**FREE BOOKS**
**REVIEW COPIES**

## HERE

## HTTPS://SMARTPA.GE/MELISSAGOMES

# Freebies!

I have a **special treat for you**! You can access exclusive bonuses I created specifically for my readers at the following link! The link will redirect you to a webpage containing all my books and bonuses for each book. Just select the book you have purchased and check the bonuses!

>> https://smartpa.ge/MelissaGomes<<

OR scan the QR Code with your phone's camera

## Bonus 1: Free Workbook - Value 12.95$

This **workbook** will guide you with **specific questions** and give you all the space you need to write down the answers. Taking time for **self-reflection** is extremely valuable, especially when looking to develop new skills and **learn** new concepts. I highly suggest you *grab this complimentary workbook for yourself*, as it will help you gain clarity on your goals. Some authors like to sell the workbook, but I think giving it away for free is the perfect way to say **"thank you" to my readers**.

# Bonus 2: Free Book - Value 12.95$

Grab a **free short book** with **22+ Techniques for Meditation**. The book will introduce you to a range of meditation practices you can use to help you develop your inner awareness, inner calm, and overall sense of well-being. You will also learn how to begin a meditation practice that works for you regardless of your schedule. These meditation techniques work for everyone, regardless of age or fitness level. Check it out at the link below!

# Bonus 3: Free audiobook - Value 14.95$

If you love listening to audiobooks on the go or would enjoy a narration as you read along, I have great news for you. You can download the audiobook version of *my books* for **FREE** just by signing up for a FREE 30-day trial! You can find the audio versions of my books (depending on availability) at the following link.

# Join my Review Team!

Are you an avid reader looking to have more insights into spirituality? Do you want to get free books in exchange for an honest review? You can do so by joining my Review Team! You will get priority access to my books before they are released. You only need to follow me on Booksprout, and you will get notified every time a new Review Copy is available for my latest release!

# For all the Freebies, visit the following link:

>> https://smartpa.ge/MelissaGomes<<

OR scan the QR Code with your phone's camera.

# I'm here because of you

When you're supporting an independent author,
you're supporting a dream. Please leave
an honest review by scanning
the QR code below and clicking on the "Leave a Review" Button.

https://smartpa.ge/MelissaGomes

# Chapter 1: The Basics of Body Astrology

Western astrology analyzes the planets' positions in the sky at the moment of birth. It assigns a personal meaning to those horoscopes. For example, a planet in one sign represents a career, while a planet in a different sign represents romantic love.

Astrological roots go back to prehistoric societies influenced by the positions of the stars and planets in the sky above them and ancient Babylonian, Egyptian, and Ancient Greek civilizations. Planets are viewed as heavenly bodies exerting a gravitational pull on each other and the Earth. Its basic belief is that these heavenly bodies influence one's life here on earth. When Babylonian astrologers and priests began recording their prognostications on clay tablets, they were buried in Mesopotamia, and these became the first astrological texts ever written. Hundreds of years later, the Romans started to write their horoscopes on wooden tablets. In the 1st century B.C., Julius Caesar expanded Rome's empire and gained great popularity by consulting the celestial signs at the beginning of each endeavor.

The Middle Ages and Medieval Ages saw astrology flourish throughout the European continent. By the Middle Ages, astrology was treated as a science that included astronomy and alchemy. Astrology was then a part of medieval culture because many people thought the positions of the stars and planets affected their lives here on earth. Medieval astronomers and astrologers believed that the positions of the stars determined future events on Earth and how people should live. In the Early Middle Ages, astrologists believed that the sun burned up evil demons from the heavens and that these demons could take the form of birds and animals to frighten people on earth. In medieval times, people thought that animals were familiars with magical powers. People learned not to look at the sun directly after sunrise or sunset, so they turned to animals that periodically go blind for protection. From this, familiars were born, or animals whose eyes constantly reflected the "evil" in the surrounding light were loved and protected.

Astrology is complicated, so it's best to break it down into smaller portions. As the Sun sign astrology is not included in this book, it is encouraged for you to learn about all twelve signs. The point of your usual daily horoscope is to highlight some areas of your personality that may need a bit of love. They're suggestions on what to work on today to improve your life or give you some ideas on what to go with

Astrology is alive and consists of who you are. After birth, the planets continue to move, and today's planetary cycles interact with your astrological DNA in new directions, corresponding with periods of calm, struggle, wellness, and sickness.

# The Medical Astrology Lens

The birth chart is used as a physical map of the body in medical astrology, and it tells you about the health of the organs and systems connected with each zodiac sign. It also provides effective preventative medicine, advising you on how to maintain your particular nature in harmony. You can rely on your astrological chart to keep yourself healthy and well.

Just as people born in certain months and years are assigned certain astrological signs, so are celestial objects like constellations and planets. These objects are always on the move, and the movements of the stars tell us much about how you're feeling and doing. The stars are constantly shifting positions and traveling through space.

Over the centuries, astrology has developed many branches for medical treatment or diagnosis. It questions our own medicine and conditions itself with science. Astrology is a science that studies patterns of relationships by observing the changing positions of stars, planets, and other celestial bodies over time and correlating these motions with the lives and experiences of humankind.

Astrology is a natural language that can explain everything in the world similarly. When we match these qualities, we discover that every diet, activity, medical management, herb, supplement, and popular wellness trend has a planetary or zodiac imprint.

# The Features

You may apply the four universal ideas of hot, cold, wet, and dry to go through what may or may not be helpful for you. These energetic properties also work to go past what is suffering and what will go naturally with your personality.

Sort the information and notice how the planetary imprints appear in your daily life. When you can avoid what doesn't suit you and pay attention to what does, you naturally align with your astrological nature. It's as easy as getting on a healthier path with your zodiac sign.

Astrology provides a fascinating insight into the cosmos and your place in it. It does not ask you to believe that it is divine power. Instead, it is a tool that helps you interpret and understand your uniqueness about the world and the cosmos. The elements are physical and nonphysical building elements of the body and mind in astrology. The four components combine to form the four elements, and your Moon and rising sign define your elemental mix.

# The Modes

The mode of a sign, or how it develops, is significant in astrological health because it allows us to express its diversity. A sign's mode expresses our basic nature and how its instincts manifest. You store energy in tension, and you must release this tension for healing to happen. Changes in the sign's mode are how the energy naturally flows in chi. Signs display love in different ways, and in healing and health promotion, love, pleasure, and sensuality can all be helpful.

To maximize your healing qualities, listen to your intuition and run with the information you receive. The planetary bodies play a huge role in the signs of astrology. Their interaction is the exact reason we think and behave as we do. Planets give us important information about the physicality of our physical body, but they also affect the mind and emotions.

# Astrology is not a diet plan.

The birth chart is similar to a lab test. It provides a glimpse of how your body differs from other bodies. It may also show any functional or structural issues that might develop along the road. It indicates how your body creates and maintains itself. Similarly, as an individual's birth chart, the planets in a cluster represent the relationships with one another.

## The Planetary Imprints

The human body has four elements: earth, water, fire, and air. Those elements are magnified and amplified in your chart to make everything easier to interpret and understand. When you know your inherent element, you can work with your nutrients to create a healthy environment on and from the outside. Knowing your energies makes it easier to work with them rather than against them. These ancient medical techniques have been used for thousands of years to do anatomy and physiology testing on patients and help determine their treatment.

In astrological medicine, the planets have energetic imprints on our bodies and minds. They are expressed in our bodily tissues and organs. These shapes, sizes, and movements are expressed in our bodies, so if you can understand these planetary imprints and how they affect the mood, behavior, and physical state of body and mind, you can provide yourself with an extra healing tool you can use every day. You may discover certain planets or zodiac signs that rule those.

Astrology reveals our mental-emotional relationship with food and movement. The birth chart has a unique way of showing unhealthy eating belief systems that may harm our sense of well-being. Astrology tells us to make room for uniqueness and avoid defining diet and exercise routines as good, poor, better than, or more harmful. Every birth chart is a unique blend of attributes, and a one-size-fits-all approach is out of the question in body astrology.

## Therapeutic Gestures

A gesture is a broad concept that may refer to any form of movement or eating style. Eating disorders and body image issues have been linked to the birth chart. Conversely, the person may have a mouth of contraction around rushed and miniaturized food, and the eyes may focus on a single meal even as other meals are eaten. The nodding head and shuffling movements may indicate anxiety during the consumption of all meals.

These behaviors may point to deeper issues, but they are not exclusive to addictive eating. They are rooted in deeper issues of social disconnect, and disconnection is simpler to state "balance." Still, understanding where a gesture originated from enables us to apply astrological notions to particular therapeutic circumstances.

# Planetary Rule

Planets represent different traits and personalities in astrology. Each of the 12 signs is ruled by a planet. The four elements are related to those signs as well. You can interpret these planetary energies by using the principles of the body's natural tendencies. Working to understand your tendencies will help you use those tendencies to stay healthy and emotionally balanced. These energies help the practitioner with an intuitive understanding of the energetic effect of planets in nursing. These views may enhance nursing practice and add holistic approaches.

For example, Jupiter oversees the zodiac sign Sagittarius, and we may learn more about these characteristics from Jupiter. There is a famous saying: "The journey of a thousand miles begins with a single step." Many astrological followers use this principle to reach their goals and dreams. I will discuss each zodiac sign's therapeutic gestures in depth in their You parts, and you can also find them summarized in the nourishment and movement checklists throughout the book.

You may use astro-fitness ideas for any activity, including yoga and jogging. When you apply astrological concepts to fitness— as a patient, a coach, or an athlete—you'll discover that practicing fitness as a therapeutic art ensures you're avoiding the harms of repetition and routine in favor of variety and balance.

# Where to Start

Signs, planets, and houses are the fundamentals of your birth chart. In the following chapters, we will look at the aspects of your chart that are more important to your health than others, as well as the areas of your chart that are more likely to manifest physically. It's easiest to think about how your birth chart works as a circle. All dilemmas and the struggles we face in life begin and end at the center, represented by the 12 signs.

The significance of the whole birth chart depends on where our starting point is about the center. Of the 12 signs, one may be the hardest climb for us, and one may be the easiest. We may be born under the most negative sign or have the best odds for success.

You'll need a copy of your birth chart, birth date, birthplace, and time of birth. Ideally, your chart should show whole sign houses. Your birth chart indicates areas where you need to focus and take a step back to grow. In each section of the book, we'll address issues that ailing organs or systems typically bring to the surface in your chart.

Planets are biological processes or forces that travel across the zodiac signs, causing change. They are not bodily components but rather operate on or direct body parts. It's easiest to consider planets as top-level influences that work on our bodies and minds rather than physical body parts.

## Natal Planet

The planets in your birth chart are represented by the birth chart, also known as the natal chart. People's personalities are often dictated by the position of the sun, moon, and planets in that natal chart. When our bodies are not happy or healthy, we may suffer from disturbances caused by the planet. The natal chart shows how planets affect you and your loved ones emotionally, physically, and spiritually. Your natal planet is the planet of your core personality. The natal planet is responsible for triggering changes you may have already experienced or will experience as you grow and experience change. Each planet produces distinct attributes that affect the body's functioning differently.

Aspects are the interactions between planets that reveal how their bodily functions interact. The aspects produce unique patterns between planets, referred to in body astrology as human signatures. This aspect works like a biometrics print that identifies each person from others.

Transits are current planetary motions that affect the planets in your natal chart. They can modify the timing and life cycle of an illness or event. The natal planet and transits show us how the planets' functions interact with the birth date and time of the birth chart. These interactions affect a person's health and disposition.

# The Body Astrology Triad

Your Sun, Moon, and rising signs form the foundation of your body astrology. These three main components of your natal chart directly influence how you relate to the world and interact with others. They also influence how you feel about yourself and how you can be seen in public.

## The Sun

The daylight hours are the longest of the year, and the Sun sign represents how you command your days. The Sun represents your vital power, acts like a generator, and you're out of the game if it goes out. Deep tiredness, sadness, and indifference in life are indications that the astrological Sun requires attention.

What you do when the sun is new and has risen reflects how you will meet challenges and overcome obstacles. The sun also represents how your body is physically, mentally, and emotionally supported by social connections and social roles. If the sun is significantly affected by the natal planet and aspects, you may need more time to regenerate and recharge than the average person. This delay takes your body a bit longer to feel fully charged for the day's activities.

## The Moon

The Moon acts as a receptor and reflector, directing energy where needed. Your Moon sign explains your unique energy use and is a big factor in digestive wellness. This sign profoundly influences your emotions and how they change over time. This planet governs your sleep patterns and nighttime feelings. The Moon asks you to discover hidden emotions within you and face the issues you hide from others. This sign sets your inner sense of rhythm and grief. Moon signs also identify how comfortable you are expressing yourself emotionally—or at least how aware you are of the emotions you want to express. The Moon sign in sign influences your Moon's qualities, such as The Moon in your natal chart representing your feelings and sexual energies as they connect to your zodiac signs.

## The Ascendant

The Rising sign rises in the east hours before sunrise. It affects how you see yourself and how you respond to the world. Your Rising sign functions as a front doorway, a bouncer, a filter, or body wrapping. It keeps the good stuff in and the bad stuff out. Some signs can rise above the clouds and see you with new eyes. Others can be modest and humble, while others may keep their heads down, focusing on the basic tasks ahead and simply getting by. The rising signs affect your intuition and your instinctual way of seeing things. Because your rising sign varies every two to three hours depending on the time of year, knowing your exact birth time is critical.

Interactions between these three main planets make up your basic body astrology. Each component has unique, defining traits that affect how you will cope with the environment and your own. Concentrate on the one that feels essential right now, and select a single piece of advice from each area that feels important.

Your Sun and Moon's house positions might assist you in determining which is essential in your body astrology. If you have a stellium, highlight this zodiac sign, even if it doesn't feature your Sun or Moon. A stellium is when three or more planets fall into the same zodiac sign. If all three planets feature in the sign of your Sun or Moon, take the other two planets' advice.

Although important, your Sun, Moon, and rising signs are only the foundation of your astrological body. The other planets in your natal chart affect you, too. For instance, Mars and Saturn send enormous pressure on the body; therefore, aspects of their life ruled by these planets make them prone to health problems. Understand the sign and house placement of these planets in your birth chart.

The Houses reflect different aspects of life and provide context. The first, sixth, eighth, and twelfth houses are all intimately tied to health, and the zodiac signs and planets in these houses can indicate the nature of a health problem or our experience with it.

# The First House

The First House and the rising sign coincide, and the first house speaks about your visible, tangible body, its resilience and vitality, and how it interfaces with the world. Find your planets in the houses to learn what relates to you.

The First House represents your physical existence in the world and how you engage with it. The house affects your instincts, attitudes, and perceptions of what life is. You can be aggressive and physically active if the First House is boosted by strong planetary activity and aspects. If something interferes with this planetary activity, such as the planets in the first three houses of your chart, it can affect your body from the neck down. The First House is about our posture and appearance and the roles we play in life.

# The Sixth House

The Sixth House is the house of daily body care and preventative medicine. It governs the venues of daily life such as your home, workspace, bathroom, bed linen, and bedroom environment. This house is about the body's systems and how your body operates from the outside daily. The Sixth House dictates health maintenance practices, replenishment, hygiene, grooming, sanitation, holistic medicine, walk-in clinics, doctor's offices, your drive to work, and your home.

# The Eighth House

The Eighth House health conditions can be more intense or long-term, possibly requiring treatment or surgery or posing a potential financial or emotional burden. The Eighth House represents your surgical history or family medical history. It details your digestive and reproductive organs and anything related to chronic illness, internal care, or tension. This sign generally affects you like a persistent wanderer or someone with a chronic illness or condition. This House is a place of darkness, and many unforeseen and unplanned surprises can come from it. It can also be the house of sexual or reproductive diseases that can damage your status or reputation. For some, the Eighth House is the house that rules misfortunes.

## Twelfth house

The twelfth house is associated with positive or negative confinement and rules the hidden realms of health such as sleep, spirituality, and sometimes sexual and mental health. This House affects how we keep in touch with They are transformative, crucible-like, and often ripe with psychological suffering. Conditions rooted in this house are often hard to understand, changeable, and misdiagnosed or mistreated.

## Transits

Your birth chart gets activated by transits, which are movements of the planets around your natal planets. The planets enter your natal points, and the planets change signs. The planets impact you by activating your natal house positions, which can influence how you spend your day, approach relationships, and how your body feels. With transits, the planetary energies in your birth chart are activated, affecting your natal astrology.

Transits activate house positions in your chart's planetary chart, as these house positions normally do not activate on their own. The planet's movement into your natal chart activates those house positions and potential health issues or areas of life governed by these Houses. These movements can present new nutritional, movement, or self-care needs. If a slow-moving planet is transiting your Sun, Moon, or rising sign, focus on the sections of the signs and planets involved. This method also goes for planets in your chart beyond the Sun and Moon.

# Becoming Your Astrologer

When your astrological anatomy becomes imbalanced, you may need to call on other parts of the zodiac for help. These therapeutic relationships are the basis of astro-medicine. Ancient civilizations recognized the need to balance their astrological bodies to maintain optimal health. Understanding your astrological anatomy through body astrology can help you do the same.

Each sign and planet is associated with an element, and the balance of the four elements is important to understand. You can restore your body's element balance by using opposing or complementary elements.

## Elemental Balancing

Elemental balancing is a great place to start, but you can get more specific with zodiac signs by looking at sign relationships. Not only does this help you understand the signs best for healing or addressing a health condition, but it also helps you understand which zodiac signs need the most nurturing.

When dealing with an astrological imbalance, know that everyone responds differently. The signs match but may not act like each other, as every other aspect of astrology has different dynamics. For instance, Aries and Pisces have a hard connection because Aries is a Cardinal Fire element while Pisces is a Water Mutable element. This aspect clashes, making the relationship challenging. Notice whether your signs tend to have positive or negative relationships with one another and work accordingly. Some signs flourish with the support and energy of others.

## Sign Polarities

Sign polarity is the relationship between the male and female signs. These polarities help determine which signs tend to complement one another intuitively as we learn to nurture ourselves through the feminine and masculine energies in our natures.

# Valuing Your Cosmic Health

As you go forward in your body astrology journey, I hope you become your astrological authority. You can use the guiding questions below to evaluate any food, supplement, herb, homeopathic remedy, movement, medical intervention, appointment, and more through an astrological lens.

The type of therapy you are looking for depends on the signs or planets you are under, the timing and application of the therapeutic, the type of condition it is addressing, and the type of people attracted to it. The material in each zodiac sign section applies to that sign in any context, whether it's your Sun, Moon, or Rising, or if it's identified as a significant player in your health for another reason.

# Chapter 2: Seasons in Astrology

The astrological seasons are another approach to measuring time, and your body's elemental profile varies as the planets transit. This variation is why, while you may know to favor one zodiac sign for life, your tastes, passions, and physiological experiences often shift.

Defining seasons in astrology is a terrific approach to understanding your birth chart. It can help you develop a keen sense of timing in your life and can and does influence each element of the chart. Here's how to define seasons, which zodiac sign is for which season, and which seasons the best support each zodiac sign.

Astrologers commonly define seasons as irregular periods of the previous year, which provide environmental cues that affect people and the things around them. The four seasons that astrologers discuss are roughly analogous to the four seasons of our planet. In the northern hemisphere, spring is the time of year when things are waking up again after winter, summer is full of activity, and autumn is when things By tracking the Sun and Moon cycles, you will acquire many essential facts regarding your birth chart.

## Solar Seasons

The signs in Western tropical astrology do not relate to constellations but rather to the positional connection between the Earth and the Sun. As the Sun goes through each sign, the physical parts and health themes are highlighted. The influence of the Sun is not equal in strength throughout the seasons of the year. In Western tropical astrology, the start and end of each sign are determined by the points where the Sun is 90 degrees ahead of where it stood the year prior.

Solar seasons, also known as the "seasonal alignment" or "Sun cycle," is the system where the Sun travels through the zodiac signs in 12-year cycles. Each sign represents a theme that pertains to your physical, mental, and emotional health. A solar season begins with the first degree of Aries and ends with the first degree of the zodiac after the Sun enters a new sign. Solar energy tends to be strongest during the first and second half of a solar season, so it's smart to take advantage of the increased energy to prepare for new changes.

# Lunar Seasons

The phases of the Moon cycle are known as lunar seasons. The lunar cycle begins when the Sun is between 90 and 180 degrees ahead of where it stood the previous year, and the Moon is between 90 and 180 degrees ahead of the Sun's position in its zodiac sign. The lunar cycle begins at the end of one lunar month and begins at the 1st degree at the end of the next lunar month.

The lunar month includes four major phases, each lasting around one week. Each lunar phase is associated with the cardinal signs. Some traditional astrologers dismiss the lunar cycle as insignificant and only rely on the Sun cycle to define planetary movements in astrology. However, the lunar cycle provides a useful reference for measuring your astrological chart.

Lunar seasons occur after the Sun enters a new sign of the zodiac but before the "new" zodiac sign has begun moving forward. The period between the lunar month and the beginning of the larger Sun sign is called an intercalary month and includes three minor phases lasting around three to three days and a half.

The Moon phase acts as volume control, indicating how loud and busy life may be, how much activity we can handle, and our emotional and physical capability. It also modifies our nutrient requirements throughout the month.

## Embracing Your Cycles

The Moon governs our rhythms and energy levels, and its fluctuation most closely mirrors our physical ebbs and flows. It also governs our ability to digest and metabolize stress, so the current Moon phase reflects our energetic capacity.

Movement is another form of stress, and the Moon phase can help us decipher when to apply extreme challenge, a maintenance dose, and when to deep rest. Understanding your Moon phases allows you to begin tailoring your diet, exercise habits, and more based on your power levels.

The Earth's tilt through the Sun's influence causes our seasonal shifts and the predictability of the lunar cycle. Keeping a daily log of your activities, meals, and six-month schedule will help you narrow down your natural seasons. The daily log should contain personality traits, events, and skews. Keeping a cycle calendar will also come in handy as well. When we reject our repeated nature, our nourishment routines also tend to lack this intelligent period.

Astrology helped people rebuild a trust-filled relationship and a deep understanding of the body. With more emotional awareness and intuitive intelligence, you gain the power to design the life you'd like; this includes creating appropriate foods for your body and understanding the signs and energies that speak to and through you. Recognizing your cycles is easy if you adhere to the basic principles of balancing your energy and taking a moderate approach to aromatic herbs, foods, and beverages.

## Waxing vs. Waning

The lunar movement cycle takes on a bell-shaped curve, with surges at the waxing gibbous, full, and waning gibbous phases and retreating gradually at either end. This change means that your food and movement need change under each lunar phase. When the moon is in the waxing phases, you experience an upsurge due to increased energy associated with a craving for sweets and complex carbohydrates. We require more fats and protein during the waxing phases to balance our energy.

When the Moon's movement is waning, we are moving in reverse. We are largely inactive during the waning phase due to waning energy levels and a predisposition towards a digestive upset. We also consume more water during the waning phase because the body is clearing toxins off the Moon's energy during the waning phase.

# The Lunar Body Cycle

Use these guidelines as gentle tweaks or focusing points for each week of the lunar cycle, no matter what type of food and movement you prefer. The waning moon phase is the time for a more liquid, liquid-based diet, and the waxing moon phase is a time to eat foods with higher energy.

## New Moon

The New Moon is a time to introduce something new, fresh, and unknown into our lives. A New Moon can represent a period of new beginnings - a beginning relationship, job, home, or way of eating. At one time, many established religions observed New Moons as times when the Gods were at the height of their energies and bestowed blessings on their followers. Many of these practices are still used today.

The New Moon phase begins the waxing cycle, but it's common to feel unprepared to begin again at full speed. The New moon is under the Air element, which signifies a period of planning and setting goals. An air element is dominant when the moon begins the waxing phase but becomes more watery during later phases. This phase brings an inner conflict to the collective consciousness between imagination and action. The solution for this conflict is to focus on what needs to be taken into physical form. You can't build something until you know what it is. This event is when the body is the most sensitive and the easiest to manipulate with food and movement. It's a good time to experiment with new foods and movements instead of sticking to the same routines to reduce stress. Try the most subtle spices during the first two weeks of the New Moon phase for the most harmony. The New Moon is also a time to give the body a rest and slow down the intensity and frequency of your movement.

During New Moon week, you should slowly reintroduce movement that feels reviving and boosts your mood. Drinking more water is also helpful at this time. Focus on playful movement, the mind-muscle connection, or developing new skills. After a New Moon cycle, your body is primed and ready for a vigorous cleansing diet during the waxing period.

The New Moon is associated with Air and the nervous system. Common symptoms may include anxiety, depression, hives, insomnia, and restlessness. Eat foods that feel stabilizing and substantial to support the nervous system as it picks up speed and sets the tone for the cycle ahead. The New Moon is not the best time for dieting or excessive exercise. Instead, adding to the body and increasing our sense of well-being is optimal during the new moon.

## First Quarter

The First Quarter Moon is like a crescendo, gradually increasing in size and momentum on its way to fullness. It allows us to take personal inventory and adjust course if necessary. It's a wake-up call to recognize when we need to slow down or move forward.

The First Quarter Moon works with the Moon's Fire element, which relates to metabolism, metabolism, and skin care. The fire element reigns as the moon begins to wax, creating a burst of energy and raising the body's internal temperature. This element can cause overactivity, irritability, bluntness, or stomach problems.

It is a good time to take inventory of where we might be tipping over the edge and take steps to regain balance. For example, if you've become constipated or the bowel movements have been looser than normal, it may be time to adjust how you eat and exercise or practice more self-care.

During the First Quarter Moon week, you may feel ready to add more heat and challenge to the movement patterns established under the New Moon. At the gym, lift heavier, lift more, or throw in a conditioning session or two. Movement is also key to balancing body energy and alleviating physical distress. Gentle movement, such as yoga and walking, is best, but any movement at this time will be productive.

Under the First Quarter Moon, the body's Fire is waking up and needs to be fed and maintained so that it can carry us through the Full Moon and beyond. Focus on foods and feeding patterns that feel energizing. Eat foods that don't induce anxiety or drain the body at this time. Eating less complex foods, like fruits, is a simple choice that keeps us feeling grounded. Eating dried beans, whole grains, and leafy vegetables will help uphold a sense of balance in the body. Relax, take frequent breaks, and focus on breathing to quiet the mind and relieve physical tension. Too much meat, shellfish, or caffeine detracts from the body's balance of water and minerals. The First Quarter Moon is also a time for increased self-care in meditation, yoga, massage, and baths.

## Full Moon

The Full Moon is the truth-teller of the phases, shining brightly on everything we've created, exposing whether or not it's what we intended. This moon phase is a time to settle in and prepare for what is to come. The body craves rest and a cooling influence at this time. The Full Moon is associated with the Moon's positive elements in the chart: the Earth element. Earth is the element for metabolic stability and abdominal recovery.

The Full Moon is when the body begins to balance itself out after a transition created by the New Moon and First Quarter Moon. Use this power to set intentions and create truthful communication. The skin becomes sensitive, and the body goes through a cleansing process. This process can cause excess mucus, dryness in the mucous membranes, breakouts, and sensations of dryness.

The brain is most active at this time, which makes it a good time to write out your intentions for the future. This phase is also a good time to practice the art of reflection to talk about personal truths and release fears. During this period, focus on eating foods that are soothing and cooling for the stomach, such as salads, cooked vegetables (not raw), and broth.

Under the Full Moon, the body's Fire is sensitive and can be agitated by too much moving, nervous energy, or too much adrenaline in movement. Practice any technique to soothe the nervous system or ease the mind. Cardio workouts The Full Moon is a good time to prune, saying no more often and putting fewer things on the to-do list. The Full Moon can feel supercharged, so work near or even slightly beyond your exercise threshold. Once the Full Moon is passed, transition your intention from intensity to endurance.

Under the Full Moon, connect with the pleasurable and celebratory aspects of eating, and befriend the sensation of fullness. If you experience sadness, fatigue, feeling cold, joint pain, and overeating, consider where deprivation may have snuck in earlier in the cycle. The Full Moon hangover or crash is a common complaint right after the Full Moon's peak. Please take some time off from the high-intensity movement. At the gym, lift only what feels light and nimble and pay attention to alignment for good form.

## Last Quarter

The Last Quarter Moon is a time of completion, where we learn to slow down and be more flexible. The body's resources are beginning to wane, and we may notice a shift in energy as the week progresses. The Last Quarter Moon works with the Moon's Water element, which relates to communication and emotional intelligence. The Last Quarter Moon is when it is appropriate to release what is no longer serving us. We don't have to dig too deep to find what needs to go. Notice any patterns that might be overstimulating or draining for you: these could be emotional patterns that no longer feel right or physical patterns that no longer work in your favor. This moon phase is a time to practice surrender, release what is no longer functioning, and embrace something different.

Quiet the mind under the Last Quarter Moon. Meditate or do any technique that encourages deep breathing and releases emotional and physical stress. Last Quarter Moons can cause constipation or diarrhea, so it is time to eliminate meat from our diet or limit the amount of red meat we eat. Steamed or grilled vegetables are easy to digest and nutritious at the end of the cycle. Under this Moon, nourishing the organs, tissues, and cells that make up your metabolic system is especially important. Eat foods that feel good and provide balanced nutrition to the stomach. Concentrated foods like smoothies detract from the healing process in the stomach. Eat slowly and stop when you are full.

Fluid is also key under the Last Quarter Moon. Drink water throughout the day. Drink warm or hot water with lemon first thing in the morning. Moving toward darkness doesn't mean we must stop exercising. Movement allows us to release burdens, express emotion, and expel toxins. The Water phase of the lunar cycle beckons us to bring more fluidity and softness into our movement practice.

The Last Quarter Moon is a quieting phase of the Moon when the focus pivots from the external world to the internal world. After a long stretch of physical or mental activity, the body needs to rest as much as possible. Schedule more rest into your day and take extra-long breaks to regroup. Some experts recommend total rest during this time to fully rebalance and restore.

The Last Quarter Moon is also a time to release the body from excess physical energy. Work with a personal trainer or physical therapist to incorporate flexibility work and movement patterns that gently encourage joints and muscles to release tension and become less rigid. Use this phase to develop your nourishment intuition, which involves perceiving internal cues as they arise and then attending to them compassionately.

Understanding how to nourish your body depending on the phase in the lunar cycle with help you live a more integrated and fulfilling life. Use the next several weeks to practice following your body's dictates with eating and movement and seek balance.

# Syncing with Your Menstrual Cycle

If we superimpose the menstrual and lunar cycles, menstruation matches up with the New Moon and ovulation with the Full Moon. For women, ovulation and the moon cycle has a strong physiological relationship. Once we hit puberty, our hormones are influenced by the lunar cycle, which will, in turn, influence the timing and character of menstruation. When we dismiss this intimate relationship, we also dismiss our hormone patterns and ignore important information that insight might offer us.

Recent research is helping us learn more about how the moon regulates our hormones. Recent studies have shown that when our melatonin drops during the night, our body becomes more alert, and our cortisol, the stress hormone, rises. Menstruation is a stimulus to this spike in cortisol, which spurs menstruation. Once menstruation begins, melatonin begins; these phases have particular energetic qualities. However, if your cycle is irregular, or if you're postmenopausal, or on birth control and not having a period, align with the real-time Moon.

# Chapter 3: Fire Signs

Fire is hot and dry, and it moves in an upward direction. The element that corresponds to fire is air, which keeps all elements stable. When the native owner of a fire element is out of balance due to some misfortune or other depleting event, the fire element's energy slowly deflates, and he may feel some heaviness and slowness.

But, when the fire element is balanced, the qi of wind flows through it freely, and the native can renew himself and refresh those around him. Fire people are fast and precise and need a steady diet of inspiration to stay burning.

Fire bodies are naturally robust, but when Fire flares out of control, it can burn you and others. When the fire is balanced and healthy, it heals quickly and provides a boost of energy.

The temper and fire of blood type A may be capable of overpowering others' feelings and emotions, but this is the strong will of someone with strong convictions. The emotions of the fire type may be very intense and expressed outwardly, but these emotions need to be controlled, or they can easily get out of hand.

Fire-type people are born with strong willpower and a strong personality. They are quick-witted and can make decisions quickly. In love, the fire type can be possessive and jealous. Fire self-care is important to keep the Fire lit but never burn out of control.

## Fire Nutrition

Astrology and the body are dynamic, and you may find yourself eating to increase or decrease Fire throughout your life. Psychotherapy and self-awareness are also great ways to balance and focus your fire energy with feng shui and other means no matter where you live.

Zodiac signs under the fire element share qualities like persistence, dedication and determination, warmth and compassion, emotional strength and sexual drive, and passion and ambition. They also have strong willpower and personalities, quick decision-making, quick wit, and fiery temper.

The fire element is one of the four key elements in feng shui. Fire is the only element of the cosmos that goes against its original nature; it tends to burn up everything in its path unless controlled.

Drink lots of water, eat lots of fresh fruit and vegetables, and use lemon and lime to freshen up your food. Avoid white rice and starchy vegetables, and eat lots of iron-rich food.

# Aries

Aries is a headstrong leader and visionary; its body systems are lightning fast. The Aries sign is an excellent athlete, fast runner, and sprinter. Aries is always on the move; its Fire is burning high, but experience has taught the fiery Ram that too much activity wears it out faster than anything else.

A Fire element requires a Fire diet with many different spices and live food to maintain her natural energy. Aries people need fresh greens and lots of colorful vegetables to keep their fire lit. Aries energy is like lightning; it flashes quickly and dramatically and then disappears. You want to moderate Aries Fire in daily nutrition so that its output is constant and sustainable by the body. Aries people can burn themselves up faster than anybody else.

# Diet

Aries is ruled by Mars, which means it needs lots of acids, including amino acids and fatty acids, to function properly. Protein-rich foods are not great for the Aries type because they need lots of simple carbohydrates; a Banana and Toast is the perfect breakfast for the Aries fire element. Aries people need to consume foods that help them lose weight, such as smoothies made from fresh fruits, green vegetables, and juice. Avoid heavy oil and fried foods; try to eat more raw foods. Too much water can lead to water retention in the legs, and heavy fruit juices can cause bloating.

Aries people are prone to heart diseases and cancer. They need to be wise about the health choices they make. Aries's nutritional priority is resilience and moderating stress, including physical stress. Eating carbs at night is not bad, as long as you eat a few more stabilizing carbs such as carrots, squash, potatoes, other starchy vegetables, beans, and whole grains.

Aries may not register hunger until it's uncomfortably ravenous, irritable, or has a headache, so have some snacks on hand that are fast and easy to grab. Pre-prepare breakfasts and dinners so you don't get stranded feeling uncomfortably hungry. Aries should separate food and stress by taking three deep breaths before meals and thanking their adrenal glands for protecting them. You may moderate your stress as an Aries by refraining from foods that create an inflammatory response in your body and drinking at least half your body weight in ounces of water daily.

## Physical Conditioning

A good Aries workout requires a warm-up, leaving you slightly damp and with audible breath. Aries workouts can easily become purposeless sweat fests, so make sure you use intensity intelligently and sparingly. Boot camp classes, CrossFit, extreme adventure sports, HIIT classes, military and tactical training, mixed martial arts, and races work best with Aries signs.

Aries challenges us to leave it all out on the floor regarding conditioning. Do a short circuit of exercises as fast as possible, and rest for one to five minutes. Nothing mirrors Aries's energy more perfectly than a sprint. Choose flat terrain or a track to keep speed as high as possible, and fully recover between sprints so you can hit this intensity repeatedly. You can reflect Aries energy in vigorous forms of vinyasa yoga, power yoga, and fusion classes incorporating cardio intervals and restorative practices focusing on relaxing the body.

Aries is a vital sign that tends to get sick quickly and recover quickly. Aries imbalances may manifest as acute and extreme conditions that aren't easily ignored. Aries is great in a crisis, but if it's creating a crisis to avoid something else or to stay energized and alert, Aries may need to make some adjustments.

Aries, a powerhouse sign, can go a long time ignoring the whispers of burnout because a high-stress lifestyle is applauded by modern society. But sooner or later, physiological corners are cut to keep the body functioning at the high level that Aries demands. Aries must completely step out of this cycle to return to true power. When Aries Fire is healthy, it gets the job done and returns to the baseline to refuel.

## Aries in the Planets

When the planets are in Aries, your energy is fueled by your drive, enthusiasm, and confidence; motivation is high. This phase is ideal for launching a new relationship or business venture. You have boundless energy that can be channeled effortlessly toward your ambitions as long as you avoid the Aries pitfall of always going full speed. When the planets are inconjunct or square to Aries, you can transform high energy into an excess fire that can take many forms, such as aggression, recklessness, and impatience. You may feel agitated and find yourself acting impulsively.

**Mercury in Aries** is a rapid responder and needs large amounts of protein and healthy fat to stay steady. It likes short workouts with lots of variety and likes to rest on the weekends. It is adaptable and can respond quickly to change. Mercury in Aries is intelligent and bold; it can think fast, strategize fast, act fast, and shift direction fast. Mercury in Aries likes to be cool and edgy and wears its emotions on its sleeve. Typically this Mercury likes to move fast, but it tires quickly and bores easily. It needs an emotional stress outlet, such as sprints or boxing, but too much can backfire and create more stress.

**Venus in Aries** has negative food reactions that may manifest as facial acne, headaches, congestion, nerve pain, or dental issues. An inadequate diet can aggravate your relationships with others. It can cause you to become aggressive with people and act out of anger because you lack love. Venus in Aries likes conversation and is easy to talk to, but true intimacy is hard to find. It likes food that is bold and spicy. You'll need to drink lots of water to help keep your mind clear and focused. Eating for hormonal and adrenal health is a priority, and this Venus typically uses therapeutic oils and fatty acids.

**Mars in Aries** is a fast metabolizer and needs more calories and frequent meals. It also needs protein and iron and doesn't have much patience regarding food planning, shopping, and prepping. But Mars in Aries likes exercises that focus on stamina and speed, so it does well in powerlifting and sprinting. Mars in Aries likes short workouts, intensity, and hot yoga. This combination is a very competitive Aries that thrives on challenges and competition. Try to moderate your output so that you can enjoy movement throughout your entire life.

**Jupiter in Aries** is prone to acidity and overheating and may experience hot flashes, excessive brain activity, high blood pressure, migraines, irritability, insomnia, and other indications of excess flaring Fire. Aries can be prone to inflammation from refined sugars and too much protein, so try to eat your carbs in the morning and protein at night to help manage this. A diet high in processed foods like alcohol, caffeine, and saturated fat can aggravate inflammation in our bodies. With Jupiter in Aries, a high-stress lifestyle makes cortisol more reactive and procreates inflammation in our systems. Sagittarius rules Jupiter in Aries and thrives when you feel a sense of fun in your life.

**Saturn in Aries** may struggle with blood and oxygen circulation to the brain, resulting in poor cognition and coordination, headaches, and fatigue. It is important to ensure that your workout program adds to your energy level instead of subtracting from it.

Uranus in Aries can be restless and elusive, needing constant stimulation and excitement to keep it energized. This energy can manifest as frequent travel, an overactive imagination, impulsive behavior, and restlessness with your routine or structure. Uranus in Aries is a rebel and can be impulsive, obsessive, and self-centered. Passion may be the goal throughout your life, but don't forget to enjoy yourself. Uranus in Aries likes weightlifting or running with low-intensity intervals and sprints. It enjoys sports that require strength and are physically challenging and fulfilling.

**Neptune in Aries** is prone to be stressed, anxious, and depressed. It often feels misunderstood by others and needs to work with a psychic medium to learn more about life's purpose. Neptune in Aries can be creative, sensitive, intuitive, innovative, and empathic. It can manifest as tone deafness, poor social skills, hypochondria, phobias, and physical desensitization.

**Pluto in Aries** is prone to stress, depression, obsessiveness, and competitiveness. Uranus in Aries is more chaotic than Pluto in Aries. Both planets need to work with guidance on how to relax and allow life to flow healthily. Pluto in Aries feels more chaotic and changes direction constantly. It tries to be in control, but outside influences impact it frequently, and it often feels like nothing is going the way it's supposed to. Implement a well-thought-out fitness plan with short workouts that involve moving quickly and often.

# Leo

Leo rules the heart, which is our most proud and loyal light. It brings blood to every cell, and the spinal cord allows life-sustaining impulses to travel like omnidirectional rays. A Leo has been given the blessing of connecting to others and allowing others to be connected back to it. Leo rules the heart and spine. This rule applies to the body that moves, breathes, and gathers nourishment. The heart is the common thread of our form, the physical manifestation of our ability to move and feel connection and love. Leo is the element of Fire that blazes into new life and spreads warmth to all those around it.

The heart is a muscle that grows stronger when exercised. A Leo loves others and is a great friend, but these signs do not have much time or patience for resentment. Leo is typically happy and upbeat and is forgiving of others. Leos do well when they set goals that inspire them and often create challenges and new life experiences. They are adventurous spirits and like to try new things. Leo usually likes sports and activities that are team-oriented.

## Diet

Leo's ideal nutrition is plentiful, fun, eye-pleasing, and mostly vegetables and fruit. It's natural for summer fare to be a little lighter and more cooling, so treat meat as a condiment and allow other protein sources to be the show's stars sometimes. The sun rules this Leo and determines its vitality. It suggests eating 1 to 2 grams of protein per every kilogram of lean body mass (so someone with a lean body mass of 150 kilos should use 150 grams of protein daily). It is helpful to work with a strength coach or a personal trainer who can develop a structured fitness program that caters to your needs.

Leo's natural inclination toward rich food and generous spreads is this sign's inner food wisdom popping up. Leo can create this fit-for-royalty effect in other ways as well. Leo can visualize the fantastic and envision how life can be better with increased strength and vitality. Life is meant to be fun, so Leos must continue to challenge themselves and live life to the fullest.

Most Leo imbalances occur when their Fire doesn't circulate properly. Magnesium, fiber, antioxidants, and iron-rich vegetables can help Leo Fire circulate more comfortably, and you should dedicate one meal per day to self-celebration and heart connection.

## Physical Conditioning

A Leo's heart is the most valuable organ in the body. The heart draws oxygen and minerals from our food and sends fluids and cellular communication throughout our bodies. When it experiences more-frequent or intense training, it can receive more blood and oxygen. It can also pump more blood.

The spine needs protection, support, rest, and movement. The spinal column and nerves send messages to the brain constantly. If the spine and hips slip out of position without proper care, the messages sent by the nerves can become cluttered or messy.

The Sun rules Leo's heart, so cardiovascular conditioning is vital to this sign. Athletic pursuits and activities involving running, jumping, and scoring are excellent for fitness levels and heart health. These activities use the largest muscle groups and contract the heart in response to movement. The Sun rules the heart and lungs, so breath work is crucial for the respiratory system. Use the breath to influence the circulation of the Fire element in the body, controlled by Leo.

Leo's health is highly attuned to solar cycles, and cardiovascular exercise is a major part of this sign's fitness formula. Leo is ruled by the Sun, and all Leo activities should involve the heart, lungs, and blood. A fitness program that works with the Sun's cycle can help a Leo maintain a healthier weight and find balance within its metabolic system. Like the weather, our bodies constantly digest and process energy, removing the byproducts of breathing and moving. The Sun is a source of life energy; like the sun, you need it to survive. Exercise helps Leos retain their brightness, confidence, and magnetism no matter the external circumstances.

Leos should use cyclical cardio to increase general fitness, create global blood flow, and boost their mood. Still, they should also put their physical heart through highly unsteady conditions to cultivate solar steadiness. Leo thrives with high-intensity workouts that emphasize cardio endurance. On days when there is not a big time for exercise, do something active for 20 minutes; this is enough to elevate serotonin levels, leading to repressed serotonin if the body doesn't move. Leo thrives on a combined cardio approach that uses both sustainable and unsustainable paces.

Leo should focus twice as much on pulling and hinging exercises as it does on pushing exercises and finish their workout with back and spine mobility. Ideal Leo conditioning is mixed modal, meaning that you use a combination of weighted, unweighted, and cyclical movements in the same workout. This training keeps you from repetitive injuries and builds strength and endurance.

Leo is a fixed Fire sign that needs consistent movement but must be challenged with varying speeds and intensities. A tempo run is a great tool for Leo to keep their heart healthy and happy. Leo is attracted to more vigorous yoga practices that create heat in the body. It also enjoys working on its body rulerships, such as backbends, spinal twists, chest openers, and postures that open and support the mid back, right behind the heart.

Leo imbalances occur when the body's vitality doesn't circulate properly and may manifest as depression, cold, faint feelings, or heart disease. Leo signs may need to reframe its relationship to food and movement if it begins approaching these things from a false sense of self. This act may manifest as a strong-willed attachment to a protocol that's not working for Leo or actively causing harm.

## Leo in the Planets

When Leo's inner light is clouded over, we see deflated senses of self. This lack of light is because Leo stops being self-generating and instead looks to others to generate its light.

**Mercury in Leo** needs the nutrients of the Sun, especially vitamin D and magnesium, and may also need light therapy. As Mercury rules the hands, it may suffer from arthritic symptoms or a problem with using the hands.

**Venus in Leo** loves extravagant displays and generous feasts but can become preoccupied with working out to look a certain way. It needs extra Fire-generating nutrients to bolster its heart force. Leo in Venus needs the Sun's warmth and light to help it radiate its magnetism and open its heart. Venus builds esteem around Leo's sexual power.

**Mars in Leo** is extra hot and can be aggravated by large amounts of alcohol, coffee, garlic, onions, spices, and other foods that are energetically hot and stimulating. It needs movement to be heart-full and inspiring. Leos thrive with direct Sun exposure to help them stay energized and strong. Mars helps Leo regulate its metabolism by revving it up when it needs it and dialing it down when it's excessive.

**Jupiter in Leo** has a soft spot for richness and enjoys reconnecting with the pleasures of eating. It needs a healthy mixture of aerobic and anaerobic exercise to ensure long-term cardiovascular health. Leo thrives on abundance and the sun's glow. It helps Leo establish a spiritual relationship with its life force so that the body feels connected to a larger sense of order.

**Saturn in Leo** needs affirmation and creativity, so use meals as opportunities to bring warmth and a lighthearted connection to your day. Leo signs may feel averse to cardiovascular exercise or prefer cyclical modalities over short bursts of high intensity, but proper training can have great endurance. Saturn governs the skeletal system in Leo and makes it subject to chronic back pain and arthritis. Intense fitness goals may exacerbate this condition but not help it. Too much abdominal pressure can create lumbar problems, so Leos with Saturn fused to their veins should practice supine spinal twists.

**Uranus in Leo** may experience weird electrical sensations in the chest and spine. You may need to drink plenty of water and take magnesium and vitamin D. It needs potassium and phosphorus to keep the blood and nerves clear.

**Neptune in Leo** may need extra Sun and Fire-generating nutrients and may be slightly weak, contributing to a general feeling of faintness. Neptune needs movement to anchor the body to its reality, and it may not respond well to intense activity in cold environments.

**Pluto in Leo** is ruled in Fire by Pluto, which is deeply connected to the Earth. Leo needs to balance its earthy impulses with cardiovascular fitness. Heart problems can arise when Pluto in Leo relies on anaerobic exercises that don't produce much heat in the body.

# Sagittarius

Sagittarius is a sign of unrestrained, quick-changing nature, and its major body rulership, the legs, symbolically and physically express this desire to explore. Sagittarius's energy is eccentric, enthusiastic, and dynamic; it loves to play and is prone to restless movement. Generous, animated Sagittarius gets quick results when its willpower is activated but struggles when the will is repressed or weak. It needs cardiovascular fitness for pumping blood and relaxing the mind, as well as martial arts and yoga for general coordination. Sagittarius rules the groin and the thighs and may feel resentment if it's regularly under physical stress.

Sagittarius should avoid deep shoulder mobility and rotational movements for inflexibility in its hip joints and general muscle tightness. Sagittarius needs a good balance of anaerobic and aerobic training, transitioning to anaerobic training.

The hips, thighs, glutes, pelvis, sacrum, coccyx, femur, sacral nerve plexus, sciatic nerve, lower spine, arterial system, liver, and left hemisphere.

## Diet

Sagittarius is the most likely sign to experience anxiety and needs a high-energy diet that includes nuts, seeds, oils, avocado, coconut, eggs, high-quality dairy, poultry, and fatty fish. As Sagittarians are Fire signs, they may overeat or overwork themselves and become dehydrated. Sagittarius can also become obsessive, so it's critical to secure food that sustains them in day-to-day living. It's not a total surprise that Sagittarius can manifest a fungal infection when it seeks too much approval from the world. This sign should add movement and fun into its practice, as it can otherwise be prone to overachieving and overworking itself.

When Sagittarius's energy is meant to be expansive and dynamic, it activates the Inner Fire. But when Sagittarius internalizes its inner light or develops an obsession with beliefs or rules, the Inner Fire becomes constricted.

Sagittarius is a physical sign that rules the muscles and nerves in the legs, but it also governs our higher cognitive ability. Proper nutrition allows Sagittarius to see clearly and aim, but poor nutrition can cause mental exhaustion and fatigue. Your sign needs to know how specific foods interact with its nervous system. Keep a journal noting which foods excite or soothe your nerves.

Sagittarius may experience nerve-related hip, low back, and leg pain. A personalized anti-inflammatory approach may be helpful, and you should explore stimulating-versus-soothing food options.

## Physical Conditioning

Sagittarius is the sign of the nomad and adventurer, and its food is an exciting fusion of cultures and flavors. Sagittarius's body and soul are nourished by eating outdoors, so invest in outdoor seating, a fire pit, or a great picnic basket.

If pain is a large part of your Sagittarian experience, it may be worth investigating any liver involvement. Digestive congestion may also contribute to pain in the lower intestines, pelvis, and hips.

The Sagittarius movement reflects its freedom-seeking, exploratory nature. It must always have the illusion of freedom, especially when crafting movement habits.

Sagittarius is a conceptual, big-vision sign that likes to get to the target in many different ways. Give yourself the freedom to follow your impulse and do whatever feels fun and inspiring at the moment.

Sagittarius is a forward-momentum sign that likes to cover a lot of ground. A well-rounded Sagittarius program focuses on lower body strength and balance between legs, pelvic positioning, hip mobility, and nerve care.

Sagittarius people are quad-dominant with weak glutes and hamstrings, which leaves the low back vulnerable to injury. To protect our lower bodies, we should focus double the time on glute and hamstring strength.

A good way to incorporate Sagittarius's movement gesture, locomotion, into your strength routines is to incorporate traveling, pivoting, and movements that change direction.

Sagittarius is the celestial centaur and enjoys varied terrain, good music, and a runner's high. Be sure to give your body areas some extra challenge with stair or hill training, and incorporate lateral movement and pivots into your running routine.

The Sagittarius yogi craves vibrant movement but also deeply desires to connect with the divine. Sagittarius yoga classes are naturally lower-body focused and should include yoga.

Sagittarius conditions arise from unrestrained and unfed Fire. When the Fire isn't given limits or outlets, it transforms into aggravation, restlessness, and a constant whirring in mind.

Sagittarius is a Jupiter-ruled sign that is natural to expand, reach, stretch, and test its edges. The most important skill for

Sagittarius to learn is how to aim, direct, and take responsibility for its expansive nature.

## Sagittarius in the Planets

The Sagittarius sign is known to be generous, light-hearted, pure-hearted, and philosophical, but it also induces restlessness and excessive talking. The slightly restless mind of the Sagittarius mind can struggle with the Moon's desire to burrow and stay quiet.

**Mercury in Sagittarius** is prone to high-flying states of nervousness and agitation, so pay close attention to nutrition. Mercury in Sagittarius people can be ungrounded despite having a strong intellect. A balanced Sagittarius program should include a healthy Moon diet too. This Mercury is restless and can process nervous agitation through walking, running, or using the legs in any other way. It must learn proper movement mechanics, or pain will become chronic.

**Venus in Sagittarius** loves to experience new things so nutrition may take a backseat to its social life. Investigate any strength issues between the quads and the glutes if you have hip, leg, or back pain.

**Mars in Sagittarius** is a quick responder who needs more protein, calories, and frequent meals than other Sagittarius placements. It will experience rapid bone density loss and hormonal changes if muscle mass isn't supported properly. This Mars is accident and injury-prone and needs to watch its work-rest balance within a single routine and an entire program.

**Jupiter in Sagittarius** can become too confident, and thinking overly grandly and grandly may end in frustration. Treat Jupiter in Sagittarius as someone dedicated to working on the attitude.

Seek balance and truth. This sign in Jupiter is all about freedom and may be interested in the latest food craze, but if it feels squeezed, its interest plummets. Nutrition is a journey, and the liver may need extra nutritional support. You may enjoy being the center of attention and feel appreciated and valued. Still, you may overdo the aggressive posturing and may often get yourself into situations where it isn't welcomed. Jupiter's expansively positive mindset can suffer from an equal amount of openness and looseness.

**Saturn in Sagittarius** may have difficulty thinking, translating, and expressing its ideas and beliefs, but focusing on deep body strength will often help it survive its frustration. You may struggle with believing it's okay for food to be pleasurable and fun, or you may cling to someone else's food "truth" and traditions instead of trusting it. You may need assistance with fat digestion from digestive bitters or enzymes.

**Uranus in Sagittarius** can end up at odds with itself and its desire for radical change. It can experience an unstable life, overly dramatic moods amid change, and irritability over small details. You need food and movement to soothe nerve pain and spastic energy. Heavy leg use is also beneficial.

**Neptune in Sagittarius** needs grounding foods and nerve-building fats and proteins to function properly. It may use food to escape a confining mental state. Be cautious of excessive carbs and sugar because they will pool as fat in the body rather than condition the body.

**Pluto in Sagittarius** can be prone to compulsive and unconscious eating and yo-yo dieting when the pressure to produce results becomes too much. When stressed or threatened, it may indulge in excess fatty and sugary foods to avoid dealing with anxieties. Pluto adds a transformational quality to the Sagittarius sign. It may increase the ego's desire for growth, freedom, and transformation through food.

# Chapter 4: Air Signs

Air is associated with communication in the world and the body. It moves up and out like the energy of spring, a fresh idea, a rush of blood, laughter, gossip, or a viral video.

Air signs may feel anxious, forgetful, flighty, bloated, cold, exhausted, and deflated. Their food and movement recommendations create steadiness while giving Air plenty of room to fly and fluctuate.

Astrology and the body are dynamic, so eating to support Air energy may look different throughout your life. What may support you now may change as your body changes. Body wisdom will guide you.

Air signs tend to be thin-boned and airy in build. Signs under the air element tend to suffer from bloating or constipation. Eating seeds or nuts with meals can ease both problems by stimulating digestive juices to move more freely. You can muddle freshly ground flax seeds with honey and sprinkle on apple slices; add half an avocado to a salad or a hard-boiled egg for an easy salad topper, or add a teaspoon of sesame seeds to your next pasta dish.

## Air Nutrition

Air signs can feel a little jittery from nervous energy or fatigue. They benefit from magnesium-rich foods, like almonds, avocadoes, whole grains, cashews, olives, broccoli, spinach, and beans, plus foods calming to the nerves, like ginger, chamomile, fennel, and celery. Diet based on your astrological element can help to balance the mind and emotions while boosting your vitality and overall health.

If your digestion is sluggish or you feel heavy and bloated while eating bread or pasta, consider eating gluten-free grains. Switching from white bread to whole-grain bread is a noticeable difference, as are gluten-free oat flour muffins or pancakes.

Air signs tend to feel the cold more acutely than people with other astrological signs because their bodies are drier. Drinking warm water instead of cold can help keep you feeling cool. Adding lemon to your water can add flavor to your taste buds.

# Gemini

The Gemini body is speedy, curious, and flexible. Geminis get most of their air inspiration through their eyes, so encourage them to take lots of naps and eat ginger, turmeric, and pineapple to provide warmth as an antidote to cool energy.

Astrological nutrition aims to make Gemini more efficient and potent by supporting its natural qualities with food, creating a nourishment practice that is highly adaptable and easily altered to match Gemini's current fancy. Gemini loves variety, so when crafting body-supporting habits, we want Gemini to know that variety can come with it. This diet means eating when, where, and how you like and not forcing your food mood to change.

Gemini needs to create some basic nourishment habits so that it can truly take off. These habits include stopping regularly to do a quick body scan and learning to read and respond to its subtle signals appropriately.

## Diet

Gemini needs to give its mind and nerves a break when eating and should try to eat screen-free. It should also begin meals with quick breathing practice, eat foods that fortify the nerves and brain, and supercharge mental activity.

Gemini should temporarily remove overstimulating foods and beverages when deeper healing is needed to free up bandwidth for mental and nervous system healing. Gemini should also make food planning and shopping less stressful.

Gemini loves blank palette foods, such as congee, kitchari, soup, oatmeal, smoothies, granola, meatballs, stir-fries, toast variations, and cauliflower, and can create homemade meals fast and easily.

## Physical Conditioning

Gemini nutrition and movement celebrate and refine its adaptable nature. Gemini athletes are experts in diversity and can move in any direction. They must maintain their integrity and strength in any creative and strange position they may find themselves in.

Gemini fitness pillars include mental engagement, movement complexity, and sports that require advanced hand-eye coordination. Breathing and cardiovascular training are also important for Gemini, as is learning to use the breath as a stabilizing force in exercise. Geminis tend to be busybodies, so stretching and exercise like yoga and tai chi can help.

A well-designed Gemini strength and conditioning program is fluctuating but functional. A balanced Gemini practice will support the hands, arms, nervous system, and lungs. Spend time attending to the strength and mobility of the wrists, hands, and arms, and explore aerial and other types of yoga that suspend you in the air.

Although there are Gemini marathoners, this sign is best expressed in track-and-field events incorporating running, jumping, and throwing. Off the track, freerunning and parkour may pique Gemini's interest. Try it at the beginning of a run or as part of a sprint workout.

Gemini conditions occur when the body's information network is kinked or blocked. They may present as pinched nerves, cold hands, and shallow breathing. Gemini's mental game is exceptionally strong, but it tends to overthink most things, including health. When Gemini is trapped in a mental loop, it can't take action and can feel consumed with options, worry, memories, fears, or noise.

## Gemini in the Planets

Whether Geminis feel trapped or all over the place, the answer is rarely to tell the mind to stop. Instead, you should ask their body what their next step should be and then follow that lead. In my experience with Gemini patients, their bodies are often eager to move but have been so focused on thinking that they forget to listen and respond. Geminis must become intentional with its body to get out of their way.

When your mind is preoccupied with worry or anxiety, check out where your hands are. Gemini loves hot topics like politics or weather, so watch where you place them. If you're holding your hands over your heart or stomach or twisting them back and forth, you're telling your body that something is off. Your body will mirror that anxiety by pinching your nerves or tightening muscles. When Geminis freeze their mental chatter and focus on their breath and body sensations, they can start to listen and hear a calmer voice inside their head that can help them make a decision.

**Mercury in Gemini** is curious, mentally busy, and may forget to eat and drink regularly. Exercise can help organize your thoughts and prevent nerve pain.

**Venus in Gemini** finds food as an avenue for chitchat. This Venus may get into trouble with fluttering blood sugar and skin conditions. Venus in Gemini loves to play, and exercise can be considered a social event.

**Mars in Gemini** is a fast metabolizer and may be prone to respiratory conditions. Be curious about foods that may contribute to lung strain.

**Mars in Gemini** is a natural athlete who enjoys high cardiovascular sports and travel. It is prone to pain in the arms and shoulders.

**Jupiter in Gemini** needs a combination of light and grounding foods and high-quality fats and minerals to stay tethered to the earth. It also needs to incorporate some weight-bearing exercises.

**Saturn in Gemini** may need help circulating air and blood through the body and relaxing the nerves. A balanced, nutrient-dense diet may be helpful. They may associate with a stuck or restricted feeling in the lungs and chest. Exercises that increase lung capacity may help.

**Uranus in Gemini** is tightly wound and prone to nervousness, stress, and neurological conditions. Regular food and movement keep this Uranus healthy.

**Neptune in Gemini** can bring weakness to the body, especially the lungs, arms, nerves, or cognition. Exercise can help, as can eating bright, fresh, green food.

**Pluto in Gemini** can get stuck in unhelpful mental loops that a small child would quickly recognize as "sideways thinking." This Pluto needs to eat whole, bright foods and walk and float through life with curiosity.

# Libra

Libra's primary physical function is maintaining the body's equilibrium, which involves many interconnected cycles and complex feedback loops. Librans can become imbalanced when cycles are disturbed, so a Libran needs everything to run smoothly.

The sign Libra is ruled by the planet Venus, who loves to coordinate beauty with balance and harmony. The way Librans move, sit, stand, eat, and breathe all must cohere to create a healthy body that supports smiling and vibrant health. Venus represents the mind and matter exchanges as Libra's relationship with beauty and pleasure. If the mind and matter are not balanced for Librans, they disturb the cycles of oxygen and carbon dioxide exchange and circulation that keep the body balanced, healthy, and energized.

Libra time occurs equinox, meaning that light and dark are equal. Librans value both sides of any polarity equally, and supportive Libran nutrition allows you to define and have confidence in your experience of balance, independent of external approval. As such, Librans prioritize the mind and physical beauty over nutrition and exercise. They prioritize personal connection over self-awareness and may not prioritize their health and fitness much. For Librans, the mind craves relationships, and the physical form craves balance and symmetry.

## Diet

Libra is governed by Venus, which means it's highly attuned to carbs and sweetness. If you're experiencing a Libra health condition, you may find that pairing low-glycemic carbohydrate foods with denser protein or fat gives you a smoother physical experience.

Libra digests best in a harmonious environment, so try to create steadiness in your body before picking up your fork. Eat meals in natural light, low light, or candlelight, and invest in appliances, dishes, utensils, and glasses that make your heart sing. Because Libra's so important to hormone balance, it's important to be mindful of endocrine disruptors. Get rid of plastic food containers and use body- and eco-friendly glass or ceramic containers instead. When Libra is awakened, it values a life that feels good.

Libra is one of the signs with the greatest mental energy. Those who harmonize this energy with food will sustain it, while those who feed the parts of their mind that fear change will burn out. Librans also have a strong heart function and are motivated to take care of their health by following a balanced, nutrient-dense diet rich in plant foods. They should avoid high-carbon foods and instead enjoy the bounty of plants. Organic foods will nourish their bodies better. Librans should eat as much raw food as possible to keep it nice and cool.

## Physical Conditioning

A scale represents Libra, and its job is to maintain stability. Symmetrical structure creates more ease in the body, and symmetry doesn't happen by doing the symmetrical, bilateral movement. A Libra's quest for dormancy teaches us that we can have the best of both worlds. Scaling a workout makes it more effective because it tailors the exercise dose to your body.

If the intent of a session is strength endurance, you shouldn't prescribe the same number and type of exercises for someone who has been training for six months and is just getting comfortable under a barbell. You can scale any movement, even if you go to group classes, by doing fewer reps, dropping one set, or adding thirty extra seconds of rest. This practice will support faster and more sustainable growth. Libra values leisure and reminds us to make space for fun in our movement practice. For serious runners, balance your quads and hamstrings and work on downhill running.

A Libra flow will focus on balancing postures, and the low back is an important focus. You can achieve balance by practicing both yin and yang forms of yoga. Libra conditions develop when the body's continuous rising and falling lose its regularity. They are often traced back to living an asymmetrical lifestyle or tolerating disharmony for too long.

Comparison is one of the most common roadblocks to Libra's health. It can manifest in many ways, including judging your diet as better or less than your friend's or neglecting your inner wisdom to follow your partner's workout routine. Librans tend to please everyone around them, but if it calibrates their internal scale to someone else's, they may abandon its needs to keep up appearances.

## Libra in the Planets

Healthy Libra energy is like a sine wave, with evenly distributed crests and troughs. When Libra clutches to perfectionism, pleasing, or fear of not living up to a certain expectation, its bodily experience becomes a jagged roller coaster.

**Mercury in Libra** is constantly comparing pros and cons and may get stuck deliberating or obsessively weighing and measuring food or tracking calories burned throughout the day.

**Venus in Libra** prefers graceful, artistic movement modalities such as dance or yoga and may need help mending its relationship with movement. Librans aligned with Venusian energy will do almost anything to keep things smooth, peaceful, and pleasant on the surface. Still, she may be experiencing hormonal imbalances that need to be repaired with good nutrition.

**Mars in Libra** can feel awkward and pause between the peaks and valleys of the Libra wave. It needs simple, stabilizing nutrition and plenty of water to stay steady. Librans in Mars need a balanced workout to sustain their energy. Warm up thoroughly before beginning a more vigorous movement.

**Jupiter in Libra** loves food and enjoys Venus-ruled sugar, chocolate, baked goods, fruit, and dairy. It is important to keep blood sugar in check and to have dinner for breakfast. These Librans are easygoing about fitness and prefer team sports to the gym. He should also take plenty of walks and reverse blood flow frequently with easy inversions.

**Saturn in Libra** is prone to stiff low back and weak glutes, which may need strengthening. They also have roadblocks to well-being that tend to come from decisions or relationships.

**Uranus in Libra** may find itself vacillating between overexertion and exhaustion and may find relief in strengthening the abdominals rather than stretching.

**Neptune in Libra** is attracted to sweet flavors but may find excess sugar aggravating. Maintain healthy blood pressure and blood sugar. Balance blood sugar, maintain consistent mealtimes, cultivate neutral food talk, pair carbs with protein and fat, watch for endocrine disruptors, and practice symmetry.

**Pluto in Libra** strives toward transformation, but its energy may get stuck in set patterns and rigid ways of doing rather than freely expressing itself and exploring new horizons.

# Aquarius

The parts of the body governed by Aquarius are less like bits and pieces and more like fields of potential. Those magic pulses, flashes of aliveness, and awareness make us human. Aquarians govern the muscles, bones, and tendons of the lower legs, ankles, venous circulation, blood, oxygenation, and energy body.

Aquarius' unique electrical rhythm is choppy and jagged but repetitive. Eating to enhance this rhythm keeps Aquarius humming in the realm of electric potential where it's happiest. Being ruled by Saturn, salt is your go-to condiment. Collect different types, colors, and flake sizes, and try smoked and specialty salts.

Protecting your genius is a pretty abstract concept, but Aquarius' planetary rulers, Saturn and Uranus, create personal authority, which is the foundation of Aquarian health. Anything that creates static in this area is not supporting your Aquarian energy.

## Diet

Being food autonomous may sound radical or frightening, but it is a normal, healthy Aquarian response to violating your boundaries. The practice of food autonomy does not preclude you from enjoying a meal out or traveling, but it does allow you to eat what nourishes you and break the rules that prevent you from doing so.

Some people want to take it easy in the new territory because they don't want to miss a thing, but Aquarians should let loose, take risks, make mistakes, and experiment with lean protein, wild-caught fish, raw foods, and plant-based meals. These foods are the indigenous diet of Aquarians.

Aquarians should take time to connect with their inner genius during meals. Put their phone, laptop, and other electronics in a different room, and don't pressure themselves to be social. People with Aquarius in their Big Three signs prefer to eat in silence or with a conversation that does not pressure or judge.

Just because you are eating for yourself doesn't mean you are stuck with bland foods. Aquarius thrives on variety, glutamate, and spicy or fatty foods. Include fermented foods in your diet, and take caffeine in its purest form: black coffee and loose-leaf teas.

Eating fish and never eating red meat is not synonymous with healthy Aquarians may need to drink tons of water, stabilize blood sugar, keep regular mealtimes, and eat protein and green food to maintain clarity. They may also need to avoid food additives, dyes, chemicals, synthetic sweeteners, excess alcohol, excess caffeine, poor food combination, and nutritional deficiencies.

## Physical Conditioning

Saturn and Uranus rule the Air signs, and Aquarius is the sign with the highest atmospheric pressure. Aquarius is a spring under tension, absorbing energy to create a release, as seen in basketball and gymnastics. Aquarius fitness helps this sign break through to the Uranian realm of genius by creating environments of physical and mental tension and then asking it to free itself.

In strength and conditioning, you want to increase time under tension as much as possible to create Saturn pressure, squeeze, and muscular fatigue. Aim for sixty to ninety seconds under tension per set. After a long tension-building set, you can use plyometric exercises to break through the tension. Be sure to do regular ankle mobility, calf stretching, and breaking up of any adhesions around the shinbone.

Kundalini yoga is the most Aquarian yogic tradition, and the practice includes challenging breathwork, chanting, and rapid and repetitive postures done for extended periods. The practice is thought to awaken coiled or stored energy at the base of the spine and allow vital energy to flow freely.

Aquarius' energy flows like how their symbols appear: in a jagged series of all-out sprints punctuated by withdrawal periods. If you mishandle or suppress this authentic flow, you'll begin to feel unwell. Aquarian conditions may present as cramps, swings, jumps, or flows backward.

People under the Aquarius sign typically learn to suppress their authentic flow early, leading to self-rebellion and a loss of personal authority. This act can manifest as inconsistent and choppy self-care habits, but they have nothing to do with a lack of willpower.

## Aquarius in the Planets

Awakened Aquarian energy is less of a rebel and more of a purist, and its most important health habit is self-devotion. Self-devotion does not mean making choices in unhealthy ways or depriving yourself; it relates to having a deep reverence for the process of personal evolution and honoring your body as a temple for its Soul journey.

Having **Mercury in Aquarius** can feel like an electrical storm in their mind. Regular nutrition and exercise are necessary to keep this Mercury steady and avoid stark changes in mental state.

**Venus in Aquarius** needs help oxygenating the body and does well with an abundance of crisp, fresh, green-colored foods. It also enjoys feeling a little different and may have unique tastes in food. The Aquarius in Venusian circulation can be poor, and you may experience water retention, cold hands, feet, spider veins, varicose veins, or fatigue from lack of blood flow. These Aquarians are attuned to beauty and often have a healing touch. These gentle, soothing people enjoy balance in relationships and are most fulfilled by a loving partnership.

**Mars in Aquarius** can be defiant and buck against regular self-care routines, but you can reframe them as behaviors that ultimately bring more freedom into your life. Aquarians in Martian energy enjoy quick, fast-moving routines that engage the brain, and exercise can be liberating and inspiring.

**Jupiter Aquarians** are prone to bloating, gas, and sinus headaches. It is important to balance your exercise with plenty of resistance training and to rely on the wisdom of your energetic and physical body to guide you.

**Saturn in Aquarius** is prone to weak, cold blood and may need more iron, vitamin D, warming food, animal protein, and salt than other Aquarius placements. Aquarians in Saturnian energy often experience stiffness, weakness, or arthritis in the lower legs or ankles. Aquarian fitness is needed to keep them strong.

**Uranus in Aquarius** favors high metabolism and consistent self-care routines. Uranus in Aquarians can feel like an inner shockwave and can benefit from regular hydration, oxygenating foods, and regular exercise that increases circulation.

**Neptune in Aquarius** has an imagination that can wander into fantasy. Aquarians can feel as if they are in an unreal state and may become depressed or hopeless. Eating healthy and moving the body is essential to avoid self-medication with drugs, alcohol, or sugar. Routines are helpful for Neptune Aquarians but should include plenty of variety. Allow plenty of space for open-ended exercise, which can align its unpredictable energy with daily life.

**Pluto in Aquarius** is powerful and passionate but needs to take responsibility to maintain health by exercising its choice and eating well. Aquarians in Plutonian energy often eat too much or lack support in making good choices.

# Chapter 5: Earth Signs

Earth provides strength, structure, stamina, and sustenance to the body, and Earth bodies thrive when they feel safe and comfortable and can perceive themselves in the world's natural patterns. Signs under the Earth element are Taurus, Virgo, and Capricorn.

Earth signs are practical, organized, thrifty, and generous. They may feel isolated and alone if they don't have a significant partner or group to belong to or are a little disorganized. They have few illusions about the world and are content with what fate has dealt them. They are known for being earthy and blunt. Their minds operate at the graspable level and are rarely free-thinking or abstract in their thinking.

Throughout your life, you may find yourself cycling among eating times to increase or decrease Earth's energy. For example, following your late riser pattern, you probably eat your first meal around 11 a.m. and then have a big lunch. Yet you may also find that before your late riser pattern begins, you stay awake all night, and your eating period may shrink to just breakfast.

## Earth Nutrition

People under the Earth sign can nourish themselves with nutritious natural foods and pure liquids. When they are young, they should consume a variety of different foods. As they grow older, they may prefer simple meals. Eat simple unless you are a gourmet enthusiast. Earth signs enjoy foods that are earthy in flavor or texture; for example, vegetables, grains, and bread, and foods that are high in fiber; the more fiber, the better.

Earth signs should have plenty of fruits and vegetables in their diet and dairy products, especially hard cheeses, yogurt, and fermented meat products, such as yogurt, cheese, and sauerkraut. Many Earth signs enjoy eating fish, especially oily fish such as salmon and sardines. These may be good sources of vitamin D and omega-3 fatty acids.

Drink water throughout the day, but avoid very cold water as it is too cold for Earth signs. Earth signs should drink warm or hot water or herbal teas rather than sodas or carbonated beverages. If you drink too much caffeine, switch to decaffeinated or herbal teas or foods high in potassium.

Other foods or drinks that Earth signs might enjoy include such beverages as fruit juices, beer, wine cocoa, and herb teas such as chamomile, peppermint, or cinnamon, which are thought to help digestion.

# Taurus

Taurus body areas are related to the senses, the brain, the thyroid, and the physical world. Venus rules Taurus and enriches it with pleasure, sensuality, love, and sweetness. Ruled by the planet Saturn, it is fixed and protective. As a fixed sign, it is focused on preserving the status quo; its energy simply exudes stability. Unlike mutable signs that seek to change and reinvent themselves daily, Taurus is content to rest in the simple joys of life and seek a natural order in the world. Under the influence of Venus, earth signs are mindful of pleasure and gentleness. They are mannerly and graceful, as Venus makes them attentive and affectionate. Taurus seeks self-awareness through others.

Taurus nutrition supports regular body rhythms and steady energy circulation but leaves ample room for pleasure and satisfaction in eating. Focus on balancing blood sugar, increasing fiber consumption, and nourishing the metabolism to keep Taurus moving.

## Diet

Taureans should be mindful of what kinds of carbs they consume. Because Taureans' bodies naturally burn food slower, excessive refined sugar can create issues with their metabolisms – and leave them feeling sluggish and tired. Taureans should also avoid consuming dairy in its natural state instead of the pasteurized variety, as its digestive enzymes may be too harsh for the slower-burning Taurean body.

Taurus enjoys eating with its senses, so make cooking a joyful experience with table settings, candles, music, and conversation. Chewing slowly and completely is also good for Taurus nutrition. Taurus digestion can sometimes feel slow and retentive. To improve gut motility and motion, try increasing your fiber intake and sipping on hot lemon water, herbal tea, broth, or other warm beverages throughout the day. Taurus people's best meals are heavy snacks of fresh fruit, vegetables, and grains. They rarely need dessert unless it's a fruit or a vegetable.

Hypothyroidism may affect some Taurus-dominant people at some point in their lives. If you need more targeted thyroid support, increase iodine, zinc, and selenium-containing food such as seaweed, fish, eggs, and Brazil nuts.

## Physical Conditioning

Taurus movement keeps the body's rhythms consistent by supporting metabolism. Taking the stairs, gardening, doing chores, using a standing desk, or parking farther away from the store are a few ways that they can burn any extra energy.

Taurus-dominant people need cardiovascular exercise, but they also need to build lean muscle mass. They should focus on strength work three times per week and do cardio once and should start with a weekly routine that's repeatable and that gradually progresses over time. Focus on the major lifts at high loads, with plenty of rest between sets, and flirt with failure at the end of each set while still maintaining good form.

The natural world nourishes Taurus, so take your runs outside as often as possible. Try to be in nature as often as possible, so you don't become isolated or overly dependent on technology to heat or nourish you. Taurus signs are drawn to long, slow-distance running, but resisted sprints are a great way to challenge this sign.

Taurus is a fixed Earth sign that loves to accumulate and hold on to things, even if those things or behaviors become toxic and self-sabotaging over time. When Taurus is compulsively consuming, it's usually a signal of disembodiment, where the sign is missing the sensory depth and connection that makes it feel satisfied and nourished.

Stagnation is a common Taurus experience. It can be caused by long-term compulsive consumption, refusal to transform past emotional hurts, or stubborn attachment to one way of exercising or eating, even if it's causing harm.

## Taurus in the Planets

People aligned with the Taurus sign need to accept their natural tendency to resist change. This alignment helps Taureans uncover what's beneath their resistance and move forward gently.

**Mercury in Taurus** may need extra help staying clear and alert. Brain food and protein, and fat are priorities.

**Venus in Taurus** is more prone to insulin resistance and hypothyroidism than in other Taurus placements. They may have a lower tolerance for more intense exercise.

**Mars in Taurus** is served best by focusing on a consistent, steady approach to nutrition and exercise and bringing balance to the upper body through pulling movements.

**Jupiter in Taurus** is prone to accumulations, such as constipation, goiter, or insulin resistance. Keeping food simple is recommended but spending extra money on high-quality, local ingredients.

**Saturn in Taurus** may avoid indulging the senses and instead "indulge" fearful thoughts or attachment to strict eating patterns.

If **Uranus in Taurus** is aggravated, eating may be difficult due to tooth pain or facial neuralgia.

**Neptune in Taurus** may contribute to hypothyroidism symptoms. Neptune prefers sensual and beautiful movement.

**Pluto in Taurus** can cast a shadow of control on nutrition, making it difficult to commit to a specific routine.

# Virgo

Virgo is an active type of Earth skilled in organizing, coordinating, separating, and assimilating. It is ruled by Mercury, the planet of the mind and communication. Virgoans seek efficiency while staying on top of things. Being of service to others is important in Virgo.

Virgo-dominant people should be encouraged to eat more raw foods than cooked ones to boost their digestive capacity and reduce the acidity in the body. During the spring and autumn, they should eat warm foods to aid the digestive process.

Virgo's Mercury energy focuses on thoughts and words and craves variety and new information. Virgo people gravitate to dieting, ninja training, new dietary regimes, and similar information. Because they are rational thinkers, it transforms material via the miracle of digestion.

Virgo's first signs of nutritional imbalance are often cognitive, such as anxiety, nervousness, insomnia, and jumpiness. If the pattern goes untreated for too long, classic digestive symptoms become more obvious and pronounced.

## Diet

Virgo needs to enter a slowed state to digest food, so deep belly breathing properly is a good way to begin meals. As Virgo's ruler, Mercury, is always on the move, gathering information and making connections, but can also make simple things overly complex. Eating smaller, more frequent meals may support Virgo's nutritional health.

Virgo should keep meals simple, with five ingredients or less, and focus on basic flavors and textures. Spicy food may aggravate this sign, so take it in smaller, infrequent doses. Virgo thrives when food is warm, well-cooked, and easy to digest. If you want to eat raw food, mince the greens finely and use an acidic dressing that includes apple cider vinegar or fresh lemon juice to aid digestion.

Although all zodiac signs can suffer from food allergies, sensitivities, or intolerances, Virgo tends to be one of the most susceptible. Astrology can help identify which foods are problematic and which organs or body systems may need support while trying to heal sensitivities.

## Physical Conditioning

Virgo energy is the lightest of all the Earth signs and can be trained to make challenging movements look easy. This trait requires strong body awareness and intelligent routines. Virgos enjoy mastering the basics and prefer simple training to complex training. A Virgo's body is more suited to frequent, timely, and directed sessions rather than large, complex workouts. Virgo signs remind us to work on our bodyweight skills before we pile on the weight and to identify and attend to our weaknesses compassionately.

Virgo fitness should focus on core development and not be limited to sit-ups. Instead, try Turkish get-ups, overhead squats, front squats, and overhead walking lunges. Virgo's light yet methodical energy translates well on the pavement, but it must incorporate variety into its running program to remain injury-free and keep its distance game strong.

A Virgo yoga practice emphasizes alignment, posture, and core strength. It's important to give the nervous system ample space to unwind and to moderate the intensity of the Full Moon as needed. Virgo Earth is like a tree, flower, or another plant, with delicacy and flexibility. However, it can be brittle and rigid when it refuses to bend or adapt to life's changes.

Although counting calories, points, macronutrients, steps, or anything else may be attractive to many Virgo-dominant people, it's best avoided because it makes Virgo more rigid, neurotic, and tightly wound. Instead, Virgo should focus on reestablishing a relationship with their gut feeling.

## Virgo in the Planets

Virgo energy gets swept up in new health trends, but this is usually a natural regression of long-term separation from Virgo's internal gut wisdom. Mature Virgo recognizes that being flexible brings Virgo what it truly desires, which isn't control but peace.

**Mercury in Virgo** often manifests as a very active mind that tends toward worry and nervousness. Focus on being completely present with movement instead of letting your mind run off.

The **Venus in Virgo**'s digestive system can be a bit lax and needs more warm, liquid nutrition. Raw food is typically very hard on this Venus, and You should keep an eye on regulating blood sugar.

**Mars in Virgo** may have more obvious, irritable, and inflammatory abdominal distress. However, true food allergies are possible, and this Mars may need more protein and iron than other Virgo placements.

**Jupiter in Virgo** can cause digestive problems, especially bloating and gas. Jupiter magnifies everything, so be sure you're expanding upon the things that matter in your movement practice.

**Saturn in Virgo** constricts and slows Virgo's body areas and may cause digestive problems, constipation, malabsorption, and nutrient deficiencies. This Saturn needs warm, well-cooked, easy-to-digest food that's fiber rich.

When agitated, **Uranus in Virgo** may express sudden intestinal cramping, extreme mood or cognition changes, and reactive hypoglycemia.

**Neptune in Virgo** can make the gut vulnerable to infection and invaders, including candida, parasites, worms, or unwanted bacteria and viruses.

**Pluto in Virgo** may have digestive issues or a leaky gut. Relax and take a more therapeutic approach to movement and yoga classes.

# Capricorn

Capricorn is the cosmic mountain goat, and its natural direction is to climb steadily upward. Capricorn gives our flesh shape and is ruled by Saturn. It provides a strong home for our ideas, dreams, and visions. Capricorn is the only Earth sign of the zodiac that isn't ruled by the planet Moon.

Life journey stories with Capricorn as a lucky star indicate a pattern that includes learning much about oneself as a young adult, tolerating suffering or setbacks related to the human condition, and embracing cycles of life and death when the time is right.

Capricorn's first signs of distress are often hormonal, such as back pain, arthritis, headaches, depression, fatigue, and lethargy. More obvious signs of distress will show if the pattern goes unchecked for too long.

Capricorn often avoids food and movement because it fears disappointing itself or being inherently wrong or bad. Capricorn must redefine its concept of success and understand what motivates its constant climbing and what it's truly seeking to reach the top to heal its relationship with food and movement.

## Diet

Capricorn food is typically cold and hearty and brings a feeling of comfort. It is also naturally a meat-heavy sign, but all Saturn-ruled signs need more dark leafy greens and hard squashes. It is one of the coldest zodiac signs, but digestion requires ample heat, so drink warm water throughout the day and refrain from drinking at meals.

When feeding a Saturn-ruled sign such as Capricorn, you want to ensure you have all the nutrients you need to stay healthy. Nutrient-dense foods are a priority for Capricorn, as well as protein and minerals. It is important to pack as much nutrition into each Capricorn bite. You can do this by using bone broth and adding collagen peptides or protein powder.

Wise Capricorn eats bone food and skin food to strengthen their astrological anatomy. Bone food includes dark green vegetables, egg yolks, fish, mineral-rich root vegetables, and nuts. Vitamin C plays a vital role in collagen formation and antioxidant protection. A healthy Saturn-ruled Capricorn diet includes organic, local, full-fat dairy, goat and sheep cheese, and high-quality saturated fats from coconut oil, eggs, fatty fish, grass-fed meat, and organic butter.

## Physical Conditioning

Capricorn fitness is about longevity, so they must learn how to pace work properly, keep the effort sustainable, and support the body's ability to move for many decades. Capricorn's workout program must include symbolic moisture, longer warm-ups, and nonnegotiable mobility practice. You must give special attention to the knees and the surrounding stabilizing muscles.

In strength and conditioning, use movement tempos to increase time under tension and mimic climbing energy. Earth and fixed signs respond well to movement tempos. Capricorn energy challenges you to pace yourself for the long haul, so you must take plenty of rest between circuits and perform exercises that simulate Capricorn's climbing energy. Create a small platform with a step or stack of weight plates and lunge back with your right leg.

Capricorn is attracted to middle- or long-distance running, but it's also the Earth sign most likely to experience knee and other joint pain. Keep the bones and joints healthy by incorporating weight-bearing exercise and plenty of Earth sign movement. Capricorn yoga practices focus on alignment, posture, and longer holds. Capricorn should warm up slowly, practice in a warm space, and start with tai chi or qi gong.

## Capricorn in the Planets

When a Capricorn imbalance manifests, it's a clue to assess the foundation. Capricorn troubles force you to climb toward something better, but navigating them almost always requires hard work, investment, and patience. Fear can show up as long-term ruts or restrictions, and Capricorn should compassionately adjust its food or movement approaches if it feels cold, listless, or depressed.

**Mercury in Capricorn** may be aggravated by stress, eating on the go, or eating at a work desk if digestive issues are present. Prioritizing a small grounding ritual before meals is often more effective than dramatic dietary change.

For **Venus in Capricorn**, food issues may show up as oily skin conditions with a hormonal root, possibly requiring increased consumption of healthy fat. Exercise, exfoliation, and other self-care practices may help.

**Mars in Capricorn** may have a rash, dryness, flakiness, itchiness, or anything else that's red and inflammatory and needs to manage stress around eating.

**Jupiter in Capricorn** may be prone to gallstones or fatty deposits in the liver. Low-fat diets aren't a preferred long-term solution.

**Saturn in Capricorn** is prone to weak digestion, food ruts, restriction, and nutrient deficiencies. Bone nutrition and weight-bearing exercise are central to long-term health.

**Uranus in Capricorn** may cause acute digestive distress, including gallbladder attacks, stomach spasms, alternating constipation and diarrhea, acute skin reactions to food, or vomiting.

**Neptune in Capricorn** may cause skin sensitivity, leaky gut syndrome, or emotional enmeshment. Supplement with bone- and joint-building vitamins and minerals.

**Pluto in Capricorn** may have difficulty digesting dairy products and suffer from chronic digestive problems. Blessed is the House of Bread, so you may benefit from experimenting with fermented foods.

# Chapter 6: Water Signs

The water sign represents moisture. Water is cold and wet, so it governs the body's many physical and energetic fluid highways, including emotions, hormones, and lymph. Water signs must learn which of these subtle messages are theirs to carry or theirs to let go. They also symbolize the human body. Cancer signs tend to be emotional, outgoing, and adventurous. Water-sign Pisceans tend to have a deep need for spiritual liberation. Water-sign Scorpios are fiercely ambitious. They are fiercely driven to succeed, especially. They also love to be in charge.

When cold and wet appear together, Water signs can feel heavy and unwell and may feel like drowning or floating far away from their intended shore. Water is most effective and masterful when given some boundaries and direction. This basic type's nutrition, fitness, and self-care are designed to anchor its power for peaceful navigation and flow.

Water signs are more in touch with their intuition than any other sign in the zodiac. Water signs receive intuitive flashes from dreams, mirrors, and where they drop things. They can also pick up on psychic impressions with their sixth sense or the ability to pick up on other energies with intuition. This intuition is what helps them to tune into other people's messages that are below the conscious level.

The emotional side of water signs is strong and intuitive. They take feelings to heart and may often go after what makes them feel a certain way instead of logic. Cancer, Scorpio, and Pisces are the nurturing signs of the zodiac and love to take care of their loved ones and the people around them. Water signs, highly emotional beings, need to control their feelings by letting them flow rather than bottling them up. The water signs need to let their feelings out because if they are not out in a healthy way or not feeling things, it could lead to depression and other mental illnesses.

You may find yourself cycling through periods of eating to increase or decrease water throughout your life. Heavy meals of saturated fats and automatic seasonings can cause a Water sign to become imbalanced, as can long periods of sedentary habits.

# Water Nutrition

Water signs need to nourish their bodies with moist vegetables and fruits, with special attention to the "wet" ones like zucchini and asparagus. Foods that are "low-moisture," like fungi or dry grains, can deplete you of water.

Use a light touch with food in winter, especially seasonings and sauces. Try also to eat foods rich in essential fatty acids like avocado, cold-water fish, and flax seeds.

Make your food choices supportive by eating weekly meals rich in dark leafy greens cooked in water or steamed. Exercise is equally important to keep your water sign relationships tight, especially your muscular system. This practice will ensure you have a positive sense of well-being. Aim for 30 minutes of daily exercise when feeling warm.

Fermented vegetables, fresh lemon and lime juice, high-quality animal protein, oily fish and other seafood, low-carbohydrate vegetables, warm spices, eggs, fermented dairy, grains, seaweed, water-rich fruits and vegetables, and well-cooked food.

# Cancer

Cancer's body areas nourish and protect the body. It covers all our basic needs: food, water, air, shelter, and love. Cancer's primary nutritional focus is to create a deep feeling of safety and trust in the body, no matter its state. This focus is done by embracing the body's and heart's vast and natural fluctuations.

Cancer gets its deep-feeling nature from the Moon, its planetary ruler. Doing an emotional scan and environment scan before meals can be extremely supportive when healing any Cancer gastrointestinal distress.

Because Cancer rules over the body's primary water element organs and systems: the liver, gallbladder, and pancreas, Cancer-ruled people benefit from cleaner and healthier water. Cancer's body fluids are constantly changing, so reducing nutritionally-processed and consumed toxins is important.

## Diet

Comfort food is medicinal for Cancer, and it creates comfort in the body and mind before, during, and after meals. This state may mean eating at a relaxed pace and easing into meals with a few deep breaths or a moment of gratitude.

For some, comfort food may also mean physically "safe" foods. If you experience food reactivity, try making some of your most cherished comfort-food dishes using Cancer-friendly substitutions, such as coconut cream or blended cauliflower and avocado.

Cancer's tendency toward dampness makes protecting the digestive fire a top priority. To help stoke the flames, refrain from liquids before and during a meal, and make your proteins easier to digest by brining, marinating, and slow cooking your meats.

## Physical Conditioning

Cancer is ruled by the Moon and is therefore highly attuned to changes in the Moon, ocean tides, humidity, and body fluctuations. Cancer should therefore use the lunar and menstrual cycle to wax and wane their workouts. Cancer's power comes from moderating yang, which means it must express its fierceness and ample space to contract and go inward guilt-free.

Cancer-dominant people prefer to work out at home, but if you don't have the space or funds to create a home gym, find the times that are least crowded and when the trainers aren't walking the floor. Cancer is a strong defender and enjoys combat sports, such as boxing, wrestling, karate, mixed martial arts, and jujitsu.

When creating a strength workout for Cancer, I blend harder and softer modalities and punctuate heavy barbell sets with yogic-inspired flow sequences or kickboxing intervals. To keep Cancer's anatomy strong, focus on upper body strength, and do push-ups, plank variations, bench presses, and other exercises targeting the chest and anterior shoulders. Also, commit to self-love and awareness as you move, and do an intuitive lifting session.

Although any sign can love or despise running, Cancer is more of a tide pool or bubble bath, and its energy tends to flow down and in toward stillness. Cancer also takes an indirect route and can benefit from a fartlek run. Yoga practice is about creating comfort and restoration, and this can become helpful for people under the Cancer sign. Use props, practice intuitive yoga, and practice Moon Salutations to balance the heat of the Sun Salutations.

Cancer conditions arise when the Cancer soul feels unsafe or malnourished or when its emotional needs are unmet. The common root among all Cancer imbalances is often emotional. Because of large emotional and physical fluctuations, they often feel they can't trust themselves with their food and movement needs. But when Cancer views these fluctuations as informants instead of irritants, it can create the space and neutrality it needs to learn from strong emotions.

## Cancer in their Planets

Cancer often self-identifies as an emotional eater, normal and healthy until they become emotional override tools. Healthy eating for this sign involves being a conscious participant in the emotions and stories surrounding food and asking if food or movement is the best response.

**Mercury in Cancer** carries a deep connection between the stomach and stress, and mood impacts this Mercury's desire to move, but movement heavily impacts mood. Exercise helps this Mercury process and gain clarity.

**Venus in Cancer** can experience large water fluctuations in the middle of the body, making it more prone to dysbiosis and gastrointestinal infections.

**Mars in Cancer** can have food reactions, stomach acid, and anger issues. It benefits from a physical outlet for any rage it's experiencing.

**Jupiter in Cancer** may cause water retention, swelling, edema, and distension. Leaner proteins, low-carb vegetables, and low-glycemic fruit may help. Jupiter-ruled Cancer may feel more at home with slow, fluid movement modalities, but it needs to generate some heat.

**Saturn in Cancer**'s digestive system is repressed and sensitive, resulting in poor nutrient assimilation and undigested food in the stool. Saturn may have trouble breathing during exercise or feel unsafe. Creating a comfortable movement environment can help.

**Neptune in Cancer** may lack sufficient gastric secretions and experience an excess amount of dampness in the body, making them prone to mold toxicity and fungal infections.

**Pluto in Cancer** is fiercely protective of its emotional needs and can be overprotective of its physical needs. Surrounding them with love and offering more support is often necessary for recovery.

# Scorpio

Scorpio rules the body systems unseen, unheard, and often associated with shame. Scorpio is ruled by Pluto, the planet of taboo and transformation. It has an innate desire to tear down and rebuild the body into a vessel that can hold greater emotional experience.

Scorpios are known to be sensual and erotic beings, but their sensuality is brought into consciousness through emotional layers and maturity. Scorpio is ruled by Mars, the planet of desire and the drive. Mars infuses all Scorpios with energy, and Scorpio's attitude may seem strong-willed and aggressive.

Scorpios need to integrate sexuality deeply and consciously into their movement and health practices to merge their energetic bodies with their minds. Sexual energy is necessary for maintaining the health and vibrancy of Scorpio's internal organs, and sexual energy is valuable for Scorpio's emotional health.

Many Scorpios struggle with issues of control, abundance, and partnering. They have much to share from their journey and are open to receiving and giving healing support. Scorpios know who they exactly are and have their own rules and boundaries, and they can find themselves passionately articulating and enforcing them.

Scorpio's primary nutritional focus is learning about the body's deeper connection with emotion and how to support its needs through mindful eating practices. They propel our world, infuse it with power, and transform energy, waste, byproducts, and experiences until they can exit the body safely.

## Diet

Scorpio nutrition focuses on regulating bowel habits, consuming fiber, and incorporating prebiotic and probiotic foods. It also caters to its martial nature, which thrives on protein and food timing that keeps it energized and ready for action. The best dietary components for the Scorpio include avocados, coconut oil, poultry, seafood, eggs, root vegetables, berries, dark chocolate, almonds, cinnamon, turmeric, and ginger.

Scorpio wants to eat because it's hungry or feels hungry, not only because it likes the taste of food. Many Scorpios are excellent at eating mindfully and also at finding refuge through food. Scorpios can suffer from unrelated masked digestive symptoms but show up elsewhere in the body as mood swings, pain, anxiety, skin conditions, or recurring urinary tract infections and yeast infections.

Hormone imbalances are a prevalent Scorpio complaint, and the root issue is often in the gut. Healing the microbiome can help with hormone imbalances, and Scorpio needs to ensure that all its detox organs are open and working well.

Scorpios may experience patterns in their nutrition, such as food fixation, control, or self-punishment. These behaviors may disrupt biorhythms and cause mental health issues to worsen or appear.

# Physical Conditioning

Scorpio is ruled by the red-hot fire of Mars and driven by Pluto, the power-hungry god of the underworld. Its exercise modalities are very passionate and intense, and Scorpios need to have a foot in both realms - intensity and power complemented and balanced by their choice of moody self-expression.

Metabolic conditioning workouts teach your metabolism to work like a well-oiled machine. You should aim to stay at 85 percent effort throughout your workout and don't do high-intensity workouts every day.

Scorpio and Aries both have a similar approach to running, and both should do threshold running to increase their maximum. Do five to eight sets of two-minute running intervals, and stop when you start having trouble recovering within two minutes.

A Scorpio yoga practice emulates the sign's trademark intensity in mood or body and may also awaken power. It may include intense sequences that promote sweating or long holds with breathwork.

Scorpio imbalances occur when there's too much retention and too little release, and vice versa. These imbalances are rooted in the organs of the lower abdomen. Scorpio's major body cycles are excreting, emoting, repairing, and reproducing. If any cycle in Scorpio's life, body, or heart gets stuck, it's a sign to reset and learn how to ride within cycle.

## Scorpio and the Planets

Undertraining and overtraining are signals that Scorpio's routine needs some help because they both lead to the same place: the Scorpio body areas become overloaded, and toxicity is retained.

**Mercury in Scorpio** can be intense and fixated on a program, even if it's to their harm. They are prone to gut bugs and may need to consume garlic, ginger, turmeric, and other fresh herbs.

For **Venus in Scorpio**, the gut-hormone relationship is primary and may be prone to estrogen-related imbalances. A moderately low carbohydrate menu focusing on vegetables, protein, and fermented food may assist healing.

Fast-metabolizing **Mars in Scorpio** may have increased caloric and protein requirements, and this may experience inflammatory conditions in the colon, bladder, or genitals.

**Jupiter in Scorpio** can accumulate dampness in the lower abdomen, making it prone to bacterial and fungal overgrowths. Regular doses of high-intensity movement can help keep this Jupiter's Water within bounds.

**Saturn in Scorpio** may experience functional issues and physical or emotional blockages in the gastrointestinal, reproductive, or pelvic system. Exercise is usually extremely helpful for this Saturn's mental health.

**Uranus in Scorpio** can disrupt the body, including alternating constipation and diarrhea, bladder irritation or urinary incontinence, and sex hormone abnormalities. Extra soluble fiber is often helpful.

**Neptune in Scorpio** can cause excessive menstrual bleeding, cramps, prolapse, or hemorrhoids. Excess sugar and starch may aggravate this Neptune.

**Pluto in Scorpio** can disturb digestion by restricting the flow of energy in the body. It's a good idea to avoid foods that require a lot of digestive effort, such as hard-to-digest protein diets or raw diets.

# Pisces

Pisces is a Water sign that governs the body's fluids and how well they flow. It is endless Water that is also changing and traveling. Pisceans are a wonderfully open sign, and while you never want to inhibit its freedom, you want to keep its Water flowing optimally.

Pisces is the zodiac's most sensitive sign and the most complex deep thinker. They need more respect for their feelings than any other sign. Pisces rules over major organs such as the feet, ankles, eyes, ears, and nervous system. Ruled by the planet Neptune, Pisces lives by intuition and collective consciousness that is not comfortable in the confines of a black-and-white world. Pisces carries a lot of confusion, uncertainty, and sometimes deception within its soul because of the changing tides it experiences.

As ever changeable as the ocean, Pisces has depths you will never understand until the Water starts to press its claim on your psyche. The sign of Pisces is associated with the webbing of nerves and lymphatic tissue that weaves throughout the body. If a Pisces is experiencing severe mental distress or health issues, its first port of call is usually the feet.

Pisces people are intuitive and easily influenced, and they may overthink and over-analyze situations, making them prone to stress. Pisces thrive on feeling connected to the spiritual world, and nurturing this connection is important to their healing. This zodiac sign can follow a strict diet, but it's just as likely to overindulge in the militant food approach embraced by imbalanced Virgo energy. Pisces people often uncomfortably straddle both camps and blame themselves instead of blaming the rigid and flawed dieting structure.

## Diet

Pisces often reports suffering from food allergies, intolerances, and sensitivities. Pisces DNA often registers this practice as a loss of freedom and, therefore, an assault on its natural essence. If you have a condition that requires medical nutrition therapy, you can still create a feeling of freedom by choosing certain foods over others and being willing to change your mind.

Pisces is highly sensitive to mold and mycotoxins, so it's important to pick through, rinse, or soak nuts, seeds, and grains and then dry nuts at a low temperature in the oven or a dehydrator. Pisces should also eat foods that support the immune system. A Piscean should eat a diet rich in micro-nutrients found in whole grains, vegetables, in-season fruits, and high-quality, organic animal products.

Imbalances in Pisces often occur in the joints of the hands or the feet because they govern movement and express the duality of physical and emotional discomfort. Avoiding foods that cause gas and that increase water retention is important. Pisces also should avoid cooled meals (salad) because they suppress digestive processes. Cooled meals may also suppress the immune system and drain the energy needed to process them.

Pisces needs more sleep than the other signs, so make sure your last meal is easily digestible and avoid going to bed feeling overfull. Pisces-dominant people should eat a variety of plant foods rich in iron, vitamin B12, and folate and cook in cast-iron pots to add more iron to their diet. They should also eat regular red meat, organ meats, chicken, eggs, and gelatin to nourish the blood.

## Physical Conditioning

Pisces is a sign of water, and this sign can be expressed through a variety of different forms of movement. It is important for Pisces to keep its body strong and flexible but also to ensure that it is not porous or vulnerable to outside influences.

Pisces strength and conditioning is more skill-based and uses rotation, balance, flexibility, and pivoting elements elegantly through many positions. Pisces's ideal focus in the gym is fluid strength, developed through a combination of kettlebell and bodyweight flows.

Foot position is an important pillar of Pisces training. Experiment with different foot positions and go barefoot if safe and permissible. Pisces and Sagittarius share a similar interest in running, which is freeing and exploratory. Pisces is a Water sign, which brings a cooler nature to its approach to running. Pisces yoga practices focus on grounding through the feet and include plenty of opportunities to get the feet above the head. AcroYoga is another Pisces favorite.

Jupiter and Neptune are responsible for Pisces's expansive and endless nature. When physical or spiritual resources expand, seep, or leak beyond the safe container of the body, imbalances can occur. Pisces may not feel anchored in their body and may feel safer living outside of it. This state may show up in their fitness and nutrition as a lack of clarity or a feeling overwhelmed by the many choices.

## Pisces in the Planets

Pisces bodies have unique energetic patterns and can feel inconsistent and unpredictable. Pisces people may find themselves self-sabotaging their health efforts or engaging in escapist behavior when they try to make their food and movement approach fit into a rigid box.

**Mercury in Pisces** is hypermobile, so use flexible parameters in workouts to match your current energetic state.

**Venus in Pisces** may have a sweet tooth or have issues with carb malabsorption. Eat plenty of healthy fats for hormonal health. It is an intuitive mover and naturally drawn to yoga or dance. It is important to incorporate some strength training into the routine.

**Mars in Pisces** has a hyperreactive immune system and may negatively respond to intense exercise.

**Jupiter in Pisces** tends to hold on to water and may cause high blood sugar, high cholesterol, or water retention. Sweating is encouraged to help this Jupiter feel free and unburdened.

**Saturn in Pisces** may suffer from depression, anemia, menstrual irregularities, poor blood or lymph circulation, poor immune response, or sluggish liver and gut function. It needs a warming, nutrient-density diet that's extremely easy to digest.

**Uranus in Pisces** may experience large fluctuations in the body fluids and may have poor carbohydrate metabolism and poor blood sugar regulation.

**Neptune in Pisces** may experience mysterious illnesses, lingering fatigue, multiple allergies, and meandering symptoms. Vigorous exercise may be helpful.

**Pluto in Pisces** can harbor serious issues toward food. Blood sugar can spike suddenly, so eating small meals and snacks throughout the day is recommended.

# Chapter 7: The Ruling Planets

Planetary transits are new opportunities, and they show the way. Planets can affect our daily life, connections, finances, relationships, and other aspects of our lives. Every transit has its characteristics, determined by the zodiac sign the planet moves through and the houses it transits through while making cycles around the sun. This transition shows when planets are in a specific sign and house in our natal chart. There are 12 different zodiac signs and 12 houses in a chart. Planets appear in different signs and houses depending on the day, time, month, and year of birth.

According to astrology, every little moment of our lives consists of small shifts, which create big transformations. Transiting planets helps us create a clear path that we can follow to reveal our true essence. The opportunities presented by transits help us to take measurements for the best possible decisions, like the ones our intuition tells us to make. At the same time, transits help us be graceful with life's challenges. After all, we need to be able to have space in our life to grow.

Transit length depends on how fast a planet moves and if a retrograde approaches its path. Your sensitivity to planetary energy also determines it. These points, for example, are used by Astrologers for interpreting birth charts. And we can recognize them in people's life circumstances.

## Mercury

Mercury rules the brain and different kinds of communication. When Mercury functions well, we have great memory, logic, and synthesizing ability and can occupy unexpected positions in life.

When Mercury transits problematic points, we are overwhelmed by nervous conditions, go wild waiting for something rather than doing something right now, are unable to filter information, and generally lose our sense of logic. Mercury transits often activate chronic nervous system conditions and contribute to irritability.

## Venus

Venus rules love and beauty. When Venus flow,s in life, we experience happiness with pleasure and harmony. When Venus transits problematic points, we have difficulty expressing love because we don't trust other people to reciprocate fully, and our neediness is heightened. When Venus transits the 7th house, our partnership partners are more expressive of love, relationships are becoming more complicated, and we may be in a complex emotional situation. When Venus transits the 4th house, we reevaluate our finances and 'money habits', and create new money strategies.

## Mars

Mars rules the inner drive and aggression. When Mars functions well, we focus more on our projects than our difficulties. When Mars transits problematic points, we experience nervous and restless states because we're not completing our actions the way we want. When Mars' energetic intensity reaches the point where it activates the second house, we become aware that we have something to take care of in the physical world. If we have a New Moon in Cancer, we become more aware of the emotional issues we have to take care of in life. When Mars transits Capricorn, the 8th house, we are more in tune with the need for self-protection, and we can review our spiritual needs more carefully.

## Jupiter

Jupiter rules philosophy and religion. When Jupiter functions well, we feel connected with the Universe and life. When Jupiter transits problematic points, we become intolerant of other people's weaknesses and may lose trust. When Jupiter transits the 7th house, we may find ourselves in the spotlight of public attention, or we may find ourselves in a relationship that is challenged. When Jupiter transits the 3rd house, we become more philosophical to satisfy our need to comprehend the unknown.

## Saturn

Saturn rules discipline and 'the practical and matter of fact. When Saturn functions well, we feel fulfillment in our work and relationships. When Saturn transits problematic points, we become stiffer in approach, less patient, and exert control of our life. We may go into fear madness when Saturn transits the 12th house, and we just feel like giving up. When Saturn transits the 5th house, we may go deeper into mastering new skills. When Saturn transits the 3rd house, we become more disciplined and preoccupied with the practical results of actions.

## Uranus

Uranus rules ingenuity and originality. When Uranus flows in life, we confidently experience new things and become open to innovations. When Uranus transits problematic points, we lack self-confidence and experience injustice in unexpected places. When Uranus transits the 2nd house, we may become more aware of our material prosperity or the value we put on it. When Uranus transits the 6th house, we may feel our emotions join our physical sensations and drive us over the cliff. When Uranus transits the 1st house, we may begin to question the societal norms that constrain us, and we might have a radical change of thinking.

## Neptune

Neptune rules the mystical and spiritual realms. Neptune functions well when we feel deeply connected with nature and often experience synchronicities. When Neptune transits problematic points, we become disillusioned with the spiritual and social realms because of our confusion. It is often difficult to keep up our spiritual life when Neptune transits the 12th house. When Neptune transits the 7th house, we may experience disappointments with our spiritual aspirations or have a more spiritual approach to partnerships. When Neptune transits the 9th house, we become more sensitive to other people's spiritual needs and more suited for leadership within the spiritual realms. When Neptune transits the 1st house, we can experience mystical experiences more easily.

## Pluto

Pluto transits two types of energy: destruction and reformation. When Pluto functions well, it helps us refine our ideas and ambitions and overcome obstacles. When Pluto transits problematic points, it activates our addictions and nervous system disorders. We may go into a pathological state when Pluto transits the 6th house, so death seems the only solution. When Pluto transits the 8th house, our need to nurture the self through relationships becomes more complex. When Pluto transits the 1st house, we become more aware of our spiritual needs and develop psychic gifts.

# Planets in Retrograde

Retrograde movement should not be confused with retrograde motion in houses. Retrograde planets may operate more powerfully, making you feel the opposite sign of what's typical of the planet's stimulation. It often triggers karmic periods of deep introspection and intense emotional experiences.

When a planet is in retrograde motion, its energy goes backward, and they stay in the sky longer than normal. When a planet goes retrograde for a few hours once a year, it might have no great effect, but when it is retrograded for six months or even a whole year, its influence settles more intensely. When a planet is retrograde in mutable signs like Gemini, Virgo, Sagittarius, or Pisces, you may feel that the planet is working through you rather than you working with the planet. Retrograde planets lend themselves well to healing work.

## Retrograde in Mercury

The sign of Mercury's retrograde motion makes you more aware of your mental activity, particularly thoughts that give you trouble, so you can consciously remove them. When people talk too much, they serve a purpose. Sometimes their words get in the way of your growth, and sometimes you just need to 'listen' to their words, then think them through for yourself at another time.

Mercury retrograde invites you to have certain new perspectives of yourself and the world because your mind no longer automatically processes information in the way it usually does. However, you might not be as articulate as usual when the planet is retrograde, so you might have to give yourself more time to express your ideas before they become fully formed. This extra time can be helpful because you can examine your words and impulses more closely and ask yourself why they are important enough to require external attention. Retrograde Mercury's influence urges you to release old ideas that no longer serve and welcome new ideas that potentially help you move forward.

## Retrograde in Venus

The sign of Venus's retrograde motion makes you more in touch with your emotions and feelings, particularly in love relationships. When you feel you can't express yourself, Venus encourages you to express yourself, and you feel more in tune with the needs of others. Venus retrograde can support you if you're trying to work through something you don't like in yourself. It encourages you to clear negativities to make room for positive growth.

Venus retrograde doesn't allow you to rearrange relationships easily because you want to honor the needs of the people you are with. Still, you can resolve your issues to become more accepting and open to others' needs. You may awaken to the need for more affection in your life, or you may be disillusioned with a relationship. You may feel a greater need for intimacy at this time.

## Retrograde in Mars

The sign of Mars's retrograde motion makes you more attuned to practical activities, work, and health matters. This cosmic event may cause you to feel like you need to control your life more. You're more likely to get sick or experience a physical problem. You may take action to correct something in your life. You may be more assertive and energized.

However, you might feel restless and freeway between activities more than you usually do. If you begin a job or relationship during this time, you're less likely to achieve much in the first six months. The influence of retrograde Mars invites you to be more present and work on effectively reaching your goals.

## Retrograde in Jupiter

The sign of Jupiter's retrograde motion makes you more aware of your beliefs, philosophies, and goals in life. It may feel as if you've become confused or your objectives have been misplaced. You may feel stuck as if you can't get closer to your goals. At the same time, all your efforts might offer you greater clarity about what you need. Jupiter retrograde makes you feel more connected to your spiritual nature.

You become more aware of the beliefs that motivate your actions and attract more people who value your views and are willing to support you more during Jupiter retrograde. This event is when you can awaken to deeper spiritual truths that transform your life.

## Retrograde in Saturn

The sign of Saturn's retrograde motion makes you more aware of areas of your life that lack willpower and discipline. This cosmic event is a good time to analyze your values, as this period of restrictions helps bring discipline into your life. It can lead you to be more practical. You might feel like you have little control over your life and that your behaviors have little meaning for you. You may feel emotionally detached from others, and life may seem like it's just going through the motions. However, being more aware of your weaknesses can help you gain more control over them. You may feel the need to restructure your goals. You may feel less inclined toward pleasure, preferring to stay at home more or stay away from other people for periods. You may benefit from spending more time alone with a book or going for a walk by yourself.

Saturn Retrograde makes you see your life as a reflection of yourself, encouraging you to work on controlling your life. It encourages you to make ethical choices instead of doing what seems easiest or easier at the time. The influence of Saturn retrograde makes you more aware of how to make long-lasting decisions.

## Retrograde in Uranus

The sign of Uranus's retrograde motion makes you more aware of your energies and your direction in life. A passionate initiation may be expected just before the planet goes direct. You may feel a need to reorganize your life. You may feel rebellious and independent as if what you've been doing isn't the right way for you. You may become more aware of your addictions or compulsions. You may begin to question your beliefs or values, and these beliefs give you direction in your life.

The influence of Uranus retrograde asks you to consider ideas that go against tradition. You might feel tempted to break away from established patterns. You may discover something surprising about yourself. Events may feel like they're out of order. The planet challenges you to change your thinking and expand your perspective.

## Retrograde in Neptune

The sign of Neptune's retrograde motion makes you more aware of your higher purpose and your need to search for meaning in your life. You may feel more emotionally sensitive as if you're more in touch with your spirituality.

You may become more aware of your dreams and desires, or you may become tired and frustrated because you have trouble finding an answer to the meaning and purpose of life. You may question the beliefs guiding you in life, which sometimes leads you to mysticism and spiritual pursuits. You may feel more entranced by mass media or movies than you have been before. This period urges you to go within and seek spiritual guidance.

# Retrograde in Pluto

The sign of Pluto's retrograde makes you more sensitive to your energies and impressions regarding obsessions and compulsions. You may experience re-experiencing old karmic patterns or being involved in healing other people's karma. You may feel sorry for yourself and be critical of your efforts to help other people. You may experience feeling close to death. You may experience great sexual energy. You may feel angry and vengeful. You may experience sudden relief from life's pressures.

Pluto retrograde can help you reflect on your choices and choose which ones to let go of. Pluto retrograde asks you to work on healing your issues. It asks you to pay attention to what's truly important to you and what you want from your life, and it can direct you to explore personal growth. During this time, Pluto retrograde can be a powerful time to push you to your limits, making you aware of unique patterns and choices that can strongly influence your future.

# Chapter 8: Symptoms of Cosmic Body Imbalance

Cosmic body imbalance can happen anytime, anywhere. Learning to notice signs of imbalance early and address them before they become chronic problems is helpful. Detecting signs of imbalance early on allows us to resolve the underlying dysfunction and restore balance to the body, mind, and spirit. Symptoms are the body's way of telling us something is wrong and needs to be addressed. An opportunity exists for disorders to be caught before they become chronic or chronic diseases. Usually, You can detect the warning signs of imbalance before they become serious problems or severe illnesses.

When the individual's body, mind, and spirit start to become imbalanced, it is a signal that an individual is not living their lives in harmony and balance. It is important to know that a person who experiences fitness imbalance does not feel any different than those around them. When an imbalance occurs, the person might experience a shift in their energy levels or symptoms that could indicate a change in the body. Many people believe that symptoms simply happen for no reason. This part can be frightening for the individual because fatigue, low energy, and body pain are often viewed as normal signs of aging. However, these symptoms are often symptoms of more serious disorders, diseases, and problems. Pay attention to your energy levels and your body's signals to understand your body's needs, raise your body's vibration, and help restore your inner balance.

Knowing what causes the imbalance in your astral body helps you understand the symptoms you are experiencing. Various body systems have cosmic components that govern their health and functioning. An imbalance within a particular cosmic body system leads to internal organs and systems dysfunction. For example, suppose you have a condition such as heartburn. In that case, the imbalance in your human digestive system causes reflux, which causes a dysfunction in the human ear system, which leads to a dysfunction in your nervous system, and so forth. A dysfunction in any of your cosmic body systems can lead to energy imbalance and lead the development of more serious conditions.

Use this chapter to define the cosmic cause of a condition, then read the following parts for help. There may be several planets and signs associated with a condition, so use your birth chart and intuition to choose which one feels the most appropriate. This chart can be confusing until you find the corresponding planet or condition that resonates with your personal experience. It is enough to get a general feeling, though. Always trust your intuition.

## A

- Acid reflux: Mars, Cancer

- Acne: Mars, Venus, Capricorn, Libra, Taurus, Scorpio

- Addictive behavior patterns: Mars, Uranus

- Adopting impulse for a pet: Mercury, Pisces

- Adopting impulse for a child: Jupiter, Cancer

- Adult acne: Mars, Venus, Capricorn, Libra, Taurus, Scorpio

- Alcoholism: Venus in Pisces or Jupiter in Sagittarius

- Allergies: Neptune

- Anger: Mars, Mars opposed to Sun or Moon in Aries or Scorpio

- Anemia: Saturn in Capricorn or Aquarius

- Alzheimer's disease: Saturn in Capricorn, Aquarius, Neptune in Pisces or Aries, Pluto in Capricorn or Aries

- Anxiety and depression: Uranus

- Arthritis: Neptune in Pisces or Aquarius, Mars, Pluto

- Asthma: Jupiter in Gemini or Sagittarius, Saturn in Aquarius and Scorpio, Mars in Aries and Pisces, Neptune in Aries or Pisces, Pluto in Scorpio and Capricorn, the Moon in the 12th house

- Attention deficit disorder or ADHD: Mercury in Gemini or Sagittarius, Neptune in Pisces, Mars in Libra, Uranus in Sagittarius

**B**

- Back pain: Saturn in Capricorn or Aquarius

- Baldness: Sun or Moon in Aries or Scorpio

- Bell's palsy: Saturn in Cancer or Scorpio, Mars opposite Sun or Moon in Cancer or Scorpio

- Bicycling: Mercury, Mercury conjunct Jupiter

- Bleeding: Venus in Aries and Scorpio and Saturn in Scorpio and Capricorn

- Blood clots: Venus, Venus conjunct Uranus

- Blood pressure: Saturn in Libra and Uranus, Saturn in Aries and Gemini, Saturn in Aries and Aquarius, Saturn in Leo and Gemini, Saturn in Virgo and Gemini, Mars conjunct Saturn

- Blepharitis: Mars in Aries

- Bronchitis: Mars in Libra

- Burn or flashes: Venus conjunct Uranus

C

- Cancer: Saturn, Sun or Moon in Cancer, Jupiter, Uranus

- Candida: Moon in Scorpio or Mars in Leo

- Carpal tunnel syndrome: Saturn in Capricorn or Libra, Jupiter in Gemini or Virgo, Neptune in Pisces or Aquarius

- Celibacy: Jupiter in Virgo or Scorpio

- Cervical strain: Venus conjunct Uranus retrograde

- Cellulitis: Mars, Saturn in Cancer or Aries or Scorpio, Neptune in Aries or Scorpio or Pisces

- Cellulite: Jupiter, Uranus, Neptune

- Cerebrospinal fluid or CSF otorrhea: Mars, Neptune

- Cerebrospinal meningitis: Mars, Neptune, Uranus, Saturn

- Cerebral palsy: Saturn in Scorpio or Capricorn. *Note: the 2nd and 9th houses rule this. You need your natal chart to determine where there are issues.*

- Chagas disease: Jupiter retrograde in Sagittarius or Aquarius

- Chickenpox: Sun or Moon in Gemini or Virgo, Saturn in Leo or Scorpio

- Cholesterol: Venus opposite Sun or Moon in Virgo or Pisces

- Chondrocalcinosis: Mars, Uranus, Saturn

- Chronic fatigue syndrome: Saturn retrograde in Virgo or Pisces

- Chronic kidney disease: Neptune retrograde in Pisces or Aquarius. This symptom may also indicate other kinds of issues.

- Chronic obstructive pulmonary disease or COPD: Jupiter retrograde in Sagittarius or Libra

- Coccidioidomycosis: Saturn retrograde in Gemini or Pisces

- Cold sores: Mercury retrograde, Venus conjunct Uranus retrograde

- Colds: Jupiter, Saturn, Uranus

- Colitis: Venus opposite Sun or Moon in Libra

- Colon cancer: Saturn retrograde in Virgo or Scorpio

- Conjunctivitis: Mercury opposite Sun or Moon in Aquarius and Pisces

- Constipation: the Moon in Leo

- Contagious disease: Mars retrograde in Libra

- Coughing: Mars retrograde, Pluto retrograde

- Cushing's disease: Neptune retrograde in Aries or Pisces. This sickness may also indicate other kinds of issues.

- Crying: Jupiter retrograde in Sagittarius, Saturn retrograde in Scorpio, Neptune retrograde in Pisces

- Cystitis: Mars retrograde in Libra, Uranus retrograde in Pisces

- Cystic fibrosis: Neptune retrograde in Pisces or Taurus

- Cystocele: Jupiter retrograde in Aries, Neptune retrograde in Aries retrograde

- Cysts: Saturn retrograde in Gemini, Pisces, or Pluto retrograde in Scorpio or Taurus. Cysts may also be a symptom of other issues.

- Cysts impacted with stones: Saturn retrograde in Virgo or Gemini or Pluto retrograde in Scorpio or Taurus

**D**

- Dandruff: Mercury retrograde, Venus conjunct Uranus

- Deafness: Neptune retrograde in Aries and Pisces

- Dental disease: Venus reversed, Saturn retrograde in Gemini or Aquarius, or Pluto retrograde in Scorpio or Taurus

- Dental problems: Mercury retrograde, Venus retrograde, Venus conjunct Uranus retrograde

- Depression: Saturn or Neptune in Libra, Saturn retrograde

- Diabetes: Uranus in Aries or Sagittarius, Neptune in Pisces, Venus in Libra, Pluto and Saturn in Aquarius

- Digestive problems: Saturn in Libra and Uranus, Saturn and Mars in Aries or Gemini, Neptune in Pisces

- Disposition to diabetes: Uranus retrograde

- Diverticulitis: Saturn in Leo, Mercury in Leo or Taurus, Uranus in Aries, Neptune and Pluto in Libra

- Drug addiction: Venus in Libra, Neptune in Pisces, Pluto in Capricorn

# E

- Ear infections: Mars retrograde in Libra or Aquarius and Pisces

- Eating disorders like bulimia: Neptune

- Eczema: Saturn retrograde in Gemini or Pisces, Neptune retrograde in Aries or Pisces, Mars retrograde in Libra, Aries or Aquarius, Mercury retrograde, Venus retrograde, Venus conjunct Uranus retrograde

- Edema: Mercury retrograde, Venus retrograde

- Ebola: Saturn retrograde in Sagittarius, Neptune retrograde in Aries or Pisces, Mars retrograde in Aries or

- Egor's syndrome: Mars retrograde

- Elbow injury: Mars retrograde, Uranus retrograde

- Erethismus: Saturn retrograde in Scorpio or Capricorn, Neptune retrograde in Pisces or Aquarius, Mars retrograde, Uranus retrograde

- Excision: Saturn retrograde in Gemini or Sagittarius, Neptune retrograde in Pisces or Aries

- Exophthalmic goiter: Saturn retrograde in Gemini and Sagittarius

- Expletives: Neptune retrograde in Pisces or Aries, Venus

- Eyelashes falling out: Mercury opposite Mars, Mercury conjunct Uranus, Neptune in Pisces

# F

- Falling asleep at the wheel: Jupiter retrograde in Sagittarius or Aquarius

- Falling down stairs: Neptune retrograde in Aries or Pisces

- Fasciitis or inflammation of the fascia: Saturn in Scorpio and Capricorn, Mars in Scorpio and Pisces, Neptune in Sagittarius and Aries and Scorpio, Pluto in Capricorn

- Femoral hernia: Venus conjunct Uranus

- Fidgeting: Jupiter retrograde in Libra

- Fingernails growing too fast: Saturn retrograde in Aries, Mars retrograde in Aquarius, Uranus retrograde in Pisces

- Fissures teeth: Neptune in Pisces or the Sun in Aries or Cancer

- Flatulence: Uranus retrograde in Pisces, Saturn retrograde in Aquarius and Aries, Mercury

- Flu: Saturn conjunct Uranus

- Frequent urination: Neptune in Taurus or Pisces, Uranus in Scorpio, Mercury conjunct Jupiter, Saturn opposite Jupiter or Moon

# G

- Gallstones: Neptune in Pisces, the Sun in Aries, or Cancer

- Gangrene: Saturn retrograde in Scorpio or Capricorn

- Gastritis: Neptune retrograde in Aries or Scorpio

- Gastroesophageal reflux disease or GERD: Mars in Cancer or Libra, Saturn in Libra and Aquarius

- Gingival disease: Saturn retrograde in Scorpio or Aries, Neptune retrograde in Pisces

- Glaucoma: Neptune in Sagittarius

- Gout: Saturn retrograde in Aquarius and Scorpio, Mars retrograde in Capricorn or Aries, Uranus retrograde in Scorpio

# H

- Hair loss: Mercury retrograde, Venus conjunct Uranus retrograde

- Head injuries: Uranus in Aries or Scorpio, Saturn in Scorpio and Capricorn, Venus conjunct Uranus

- Headaches: Saturn opposite Jupiter or the Moon, Saturn and Mercury in Aries or Scorpio, Jupiter in Leo or Virgo, Neptune in Aries or Pisces, Mercury in Gemini

- Hearing loss: Neptune retrograde in Aries or Pisces, Mars retrograde in Scorpio or Aries, Pluto retrograde in Scorpio

- Heart disease: Saturn conjunct Uranus or Pluto, Saturn retrograde in Scorpio or Capricorn, Neptune retrograde in Pisces, Mars retrograde in Aries

- Heartburn: Mars in Aries and Pluto

- High blood pressure: Saturn in Libra and Uranus

- HIV: Neptune retrograde in Aries or Pisces, Saturn retrograde opposite Uranus retrograde in Scorpio or Sagittarius, Jupiter retrograde opposite Neptune retrograde in Scorpio or Sagittarius, Saturn retrograde in Scorpio and Capricorn, Jupiter retrograde opposite Neptune retrograde in Scorpio and Sagittarius

- Hives: Mars in Libra, Pluto, Saturn

- Hot flashes/flashes: Mercury conjunct Jupiter, Saturn opposite the Sun

- Hysteria: Mars, Venus in Libra

I

- Impotence: Saturn conjunct Uranus or Pluto, Mars in Libra and Aquarius or Capricorn, Uranus in Aries or Libra

- Insomnia: Mercury in Gemini, Aries, Sagittarius and Scorpio, Saturn opposite Uranus, Pluto in Aquarius

- Irritable bowel syndrome: Mars, Saturn, Neptune or Pluto in Libra, Uranus, Venus opposite Saturn or Neptune, Mercury conjunct Saturn or Neptune

- Ischemic heart disease or heart attack: Saturn or Neptune retrograde in Libra, Saturn opposite Jupiter retrograde in Libra, Saturn retrograde in Libra or Aquarius, Saturn opposite the Sun in Virgo, Saturn opposite the Moon in Leo, Mars opposite Jupiter retrograde or the Sun or Moon, Mars conjunct Jupiter retrograde or the Sun or Moon, Mars opposite the Sun

# J

- Jaw stiffness: Saturn opposite the Moon

- Jet lag: Saturn in Aquarius or Scorpio, Mars in Libra or Aries, Neptune in Pisces

- Joint pain: Saturn conjuncts Uranus or Pluto in Scorpio and Capricorn, Neptune conjuncts Pluto and the Sun or Moon opposite Uranus

- JRA / Juvenile arthritis: Saturn retrograde in Virgo or Pisces

# K

- Kidney stones: Neptune in Taurus or Pisces, Jupiter

- Knock-knees: Jupiter in Taurus or Libra

- Knee surgery: Neptune conjunct Pluto

# L

- Laryngitis: Neptune or Jupiter in Pisces

- Lead poisoning: Jupiter in Virgo

- Leg cramps and spasms: Saturn conjunct Uranus or Pluto

- Liver disease: Saturn in Libra and Uranus

- Lung cancer: Neptune in Taurus or Pisces, Uranus in Aries or Libra, Saturn conjunct Uranus

- Lymphoma: Mars opposing Sun or Moon in Aries or Scorpio, Neptune in Taurus or Pisces, Jupiter

**M**

- Mass, cancer: Neptune in Taurus or Pisces, Jupiter

- Mastitis: Neptune in Taurus or Pisces, Mercury conjunct Saturn, Mars opposite Moon, Uranus in Leo or Libra, Saturn

- Mental illness: Saturn in Libra and Uranus, Neptune in Taurus or Pisces, Jupiter

- Migraine headaches: Saturn opposite the Sun

- Menstrual cramps: Saturn opposite or square the Sun or Moon, Neptune in Taurus or Pisces, Mars conjunct Uranus

- Mucocele: Pluto retrograde in Scorpio and Capricorn

- Multiple Sclerosis: Uranus in Libra

- Muscle cramps or fasciculation: Neptune in Aries or Pisces

**N**

- Nail fungus: Venus retrograde, Mercury retrograde, Mercury conjunct Uranus retrograde

- Nausea and vomiting: Mars opposite the Sun or Moon, Uranus in Aries or Libra, Neptune in Taurus or Pisces, Mars conjunct Uranus retrograde

- Neck pain: Saturn conjunct Uranus or Pluto, Saturn retrograde in Aries, Libra and Aquarius, Mercury retrograde opposite Uranus retrograde in Scorpio or Sagittarius

- Neuritis: Neptune retrograde in Aries or Scorpio

- Nephritis: Neptune retrograde in Aries and Scorpio

- Neuropathy: Neptune retrograde in Aries and Scorpio, Saturn in Libra and Uranus, Venus in Gemini or Libra

# O

- Obesity: Neptune in Taurus or Pisces

- Ocular histoplasmosis: Neptune in Aries or Pisces, Jupiter, Pluto retrograde

- Ovarian cysts or an ovarian tumor: Neptune in Taurus or Pisces, Uranus retrograde in Aries and Libra, Saturn retrograde in Scorpio and Capricorn

- Osteoporosis: Saturn retrograde in Virgo or Scorpio, Neptune retrograde in Pisces

- Otitis media, mastoiditis: Neptune retrograde in Aries or Pisces

- Otitis external: Mas retrograde in Libra, Taurus or Aquarius, Uranus retrograde in Aries or Libra, Jupiter retrograde in Libra or Taurus

# P

- Palmar erythema, or reddening of the palms: Neptune in reverse motion, Neptune retrograde in Aries or Pisces, Jupiter retrograde in Scorpio

- Panic attacks: Saturn opposite the Sun in Virgo

- Paralysis: Neptune in Aries or Pisces, Venus opposite the Sun or Moon

- Paraplegia: Saturn in Scorpio and Capricorn, Venus, Jupiter

- Pancreatic cancer: Jupiter retrograde in Sagittarius or Pisces

- Paralysis of any type: Saturn opposite the Moon or Jupiter

- Parasomnia, sleepwalking: Mars retrograde in Libra, Uranus retrograde in Leo or Libra

- Peripheral vascular disease: Saturn

- Pneumothorax: Puto retrograde in Scorpio and Capricorn

- Pneumonia: Neptune retrograde in Aries or Pisces, Uranus retrograde in Leo and Aquarius, Saturn retrograde in Scorpio and Capricorn

- Psoriasis: Neptune retrograde in Taurus or Pisces, Uranus retrograde in Aries and Libra, Saturn retrograde in Scorpio and Capricorn

- Pulmonary disease: Pluto retrograde in Scorpio and Capricorn

- Pyoderma gangrenosum: Saturn retrograde in Scorpio and Capricorn, Neptune retrograde in Taurus or Pisces, Uranus retrograde in Leo and Aquarius

# Q

- Q fever: Pluto retrograde in Scorpio and Capricorn

# R

- Radiation poisoning or radiation injury: Saturn and Pluto retrograde in Scorpio and Capricorn, Neptune retrograde

- Restless leg syndrome: Mercury opposite the Sun and Moon, Mars opposite the Sun

- Rheumatic fever: Mars opposite the Sun or Moon in Aries or Scorpio

- Rheumatoid arthritis: Mars opposite the Sun or Moon in Aries or Scorpio

- Ringworm infection: Mercury retrograde

- Rosacea: Neptune retrograde in Aries or Pisces, Mars retrograde in Scorpio and Aries, Pluto retrograde in Scorpio and Capricorn, Saturn retrograde in Scorpio and Capricorn

- Rubella: Neptune retrograde in Aries or Pisces, Uranus retrograde in Leo and Aquarius, Saturn retrograde in Scorpio

- RSD or Reflex sympathetic dystrophy: Saturn retrograde in Scorpio and Capricorn, Neptune retrograde in Taurus or Pisces, Uranus retrograde in Leo and Aquarius

**S**

- Sad songs, music, and poetry: Mars opposite the Sun or Moon in Libra and Aquarius, Jupiter opposite the Sun or Moon in Taurus or Libra, Saturn retrograde in Libra and Scorpio, Uranus retrograde in Leo, Jupiter retrograde in Sagittarius, Saturn retrograde in Scorpio and Capricorn

- Sarcoma: Pluto retrograde in Scorpio and Capricorn, Saturn retrograde in Scorpio and Capricorn, Uranus retrograde in Leo, Jupiter retrograde in Sagittarius, Saturn retrograde in Scorpio and Capricorn

- Scabies: Jupiter retrograde in Scorpio and Libra, Venus retrograde, Uranus retrograde

- Scarlet fever: Neptune retrograde in Aries or Pisces, Uranus retrograde in Leo, Jupiter retrograde in Sagittarius, Saturn retrograde in Scorpio and Capricorn

- Schizophrenia: Mars in Libra opposite Neptune retrograde and Jupiter retrograde, Saturn retrograde opposite Uranus retrograde and Pluto retrograde in Horoscope sign Libra

- Scleritis: Neptune retrograde in Scorpio or Sagittarius, Jupiter retrograde in Scorpio or Sagittarius

- Scurvy: Neptune retrograde in Taurus or Pisces, Jupiter retrograde in Scorpio, Saturn retrograde

- Seborrheic dermatitis: Uranus retrograde in Leo

- Seizures: Sturn in Libra and Uranus, Uranus retrograde in Leo, Saturn retrograde and Uranus retrograde in Libra, Uranus retrograde in Leo, Saturn retrograde and Uranus retrograde in Aries, Neptune retrograde in Taurus and Pisces, Jupiter retrograde in Libra, Mars retrograde in Libra and Aquarius, Venus retrograde in Virgo, Jupiter retrograde opposite to Neptune retrograde in Scorpio

- Septicemia: Neptune retrograde in Aries or Pisces

- Sex addiction: Neptune in Aries or Pisces

- Shingles: Neptune retrograde in Aries or Pisces, Jupiter retrograde

- Sinusitis: Jupiter retrograde in Scorpio and Libra, Saturn retrograde in Scorpio and Capricorn, Uranus retrograde in Scorpio and Aries

- Skin cancer: Saturn retrograde in Scorpio and Capricorn, Jupiter retrograde in Scorpio and Libra, Venus retrograde in Virgo, Saturn retrograde conjunct Uranus retrograde, Jupiter retrograde conjunct Uranus retrograde

- Skin rashes: Neptune in Aries or Pisces, Jupiter retrograde in Scorpio and Taurus, Neptune retrograde conjunct Uranus retrograde, Jupiter retrograde conjunct Uranus retrograde

- Skin ulcers: Saturn retrograde in Scorpio and Capricorn

- Sleep apnea: Saturn opposite the North Node

- Sleepwalking: Mars retrograde in Libra and Aquarius, Venus retrograde, Jupiter retrograde, Uranus retrograde

- Smallpox: Saturn opposite the Sun and Moon, Pluto opposite the Sun and Moon, Jupiter opposite the Sun and Moon, Uranus opposite the Sun and Moon, Neptune opposite the Sun and Moon, Mars opposite the Sun and

Moon, Venus opposite the Sun and Moon, Saturn retrograde conjunct Uranus retrograde, Neptune retrograde conjunct Uranus retrograde, Jupiter retrograde conjunct Uranus retrograde

- Smoking-related illnesses: Saturn retrograde in Scorpio and Capricorn, Jupiter retrograde opposite Neptune retrograde in Scorpio and Scorpio

- Spastic cerebral palsy: Pluto retrograde in Scorpio and Capricorn, Saturn retrograde in Scorpio and Capricorn

- Squamous cell carcinoma: Saturn retrograde in Scorpio and Capricorn, Mars retrograde in Libra and Aquarius, Neptune retrograde in Aries or Pisces, Uranus retrograde in Leo

- Spinal cord injury: Saturn retrograde in Scorpio and Capricorn

- Stroke: Saturn retrograde opposite Uranus retrograde, Saturn retrograde opposite Neptune retrograde

## T

- Taeniasis: Pluto retrograde in Scorpio and Capricorn, Saturn retrograde in Scorpio and Capricorn, Uranus retrograde in Leo and Aquarius, Jupiter retrograde in Scorpio and Libra, Neptune retrograde in Taurus or Pisces, Mars retrograde in Scorpio and Aquarius

- Tetanus: Saturn opposite the Sun and Moon

- Thyrotoxicosis: Neptune retrograde in Aries or Pisces, Mars retrograde in Libra and Aquarius, Saturn retrograde in Capricorn, Jupiter retrograde in Scorpio or Sagittarius

- Tinea versicolor: Saturn retrograde in Scorpio and Capricorn, Uranus retrograde in Leo and Aquarius, Mars retrograde in Scorpio and Aquarius, Neptune retrograde conjunct Uranus retrograde, Jupiter retrograde conjunct Uranus retrograde

- Tourette syndrome: Mars reverse in Libra and Aquarius, Saturn retrograde conjunct Uranus

- Toxoplasmosis: Neptune retrograde in Aries or Pisces, Uranus retrograde in Leo and Aquarius

- Transmissible spongiform encephalopathy: Saturn opposite the Sun and Moon

- Tularemia: Pluto retrograde in Scorpio and Capricorn, Saturn retrograde in the same signs, Jupiter retrograde in Scorpio and Libra, Neptune retrograde in Taurus or Pisces

# U

- Ulcers: Saturn retrograde in Scorpio and Capricorn, Uranus retrograde in Leo and Aquarius, Neptune retrograde in Aries or Pisces, Mars retrograde in Libra and Capricorn

- Ulcers of the lower esophagus: Saturn retrograde in Scorpio and Capricorn, Mars retrograde in Libra and Aquarius, Uranus retrograde in Leo and Aquarius

- Urinary tract infection or UTI: Neptune retrograde in Aries or Pisces, Uranus retrograde in Leo and Aquarius, Saturn retrograde in Scorpio and Capricorn, Mars retrograde in Libra and Capricorn, Jupiter retrograde in Scorpio and Libra

# V

- Varicose veins: Saturn retrograde in Scorpio and Capricorn

- Vasculitis: Saturn retrograde in Scorpio and Capricorn, Pluto retrograde in Scorpio and Capricorn, Jupiter retrograde in Scorpio and Libra, Saturn retrograde in Scorpio and Capricorn

- V.D.: Neptune in Aries or Pisces, Saturn retrograde opposite Uranus retrograde

- Vertigo: Saturn retrograde in Scorpio and Capricorn, Neptune retrograde in Aries or Pisces, Jupiter retrograde in Scorpio and Libra, Jupiter retrograde opposite to Neptune retrograde in Scorpio and Scorpio

- Viral infection: Neptune retrograde and Jupiter retrograde, Pluto retrograde opposite Uranus retrograde in the Horoscope sign Aries

- Vulvodynia: Neptune retrograde in Aries or Pisces. Saturn retrograde in Scorpio and Capricorn

- Vulvovaginitis: Saturn retrograde in Scorpio and Capricorn, Neptune retrograde in Aries or Pisces, Uranus retrograde opposite Pluto retrograde in Scorpio and Sagittarius, Jupiter retrograde opposite Neptune retrograde in Scorpio and Sagittarius, Saturn retrograde in Scorpio and Capricorn, Mars retrograde in Libra and Capricorn

**W**

- West Nile virus: Neptune retrograde in Aries or Pisces, Jupiter retrograde in Scorpio and Libra, Saturn retrograde in Scorpio and Capricorn, Uranus retrograde opposite Pluto retrograde in Scorpio and Sagittarius

- White cell disease, leukemia: Neptune retrograde in Aries or Pisces, Jupiter retrograde in Scorpio and Libra, Saturn retrograde in Scorpio and Capricorn, Uranus retrograde opposite Pluto retrograde in Scorpio and Sagittarius

**Y**

- Yellow fever: Neptune retrograde in Aries or Pisces, Jupiter retrograde in Scorpio and Libra

**Z**

- ZIKA virus: Pluto retrograde in Scorpio and Capricorn, Jupiter retrograde in Scorpio and Libra

# Chapter 9: Astrological Terms

Here are some commonly used terms in body astrology. These terms are used more often than others to discuss a chart or a person's life journey, so it's a good idea to understand what they mean. There are variations in the interpretation of these terms, and I do not guarantee that my understanding of them is completely accurate. I welcome corrections. Where there is variation in the meaning, I indicate this.

**Eastern modality:** The sign of the rising is East. The birth chart or astrological portrait is usually oriented so that the rising sign is uppermost.

**Western modality:** The rising sign is North. Because of recent changes in the equinoxes etc., most astrologers who perform spoken and written consultations now orient the body of a person's birth chart so that North is for the rising sign.

**Rising:** This is the direction of the Ascendant sign. This sign is found on the Eastern horizon at the time of birth. It is commonly called the Ascendant. The rising sign determines the chart's rising energy. Sun Sign: This is the sign the sun is at the particular time you were born.

**Conjunction:** This occurs when two or more planets, or points, are almost exactly on the same degree, or 0°, or the same degree apart by a minimal distance. The minimal distance varies somewhat between astrologers.

**Opposition:** The act of having two planets close together in the sky. It is a sign of power struggles, friction, and conflict.

**Square:** These are two planets placed 90 degrees away or vertically stacked. It is a sign of effort and frustration toward a goal.

**Sextile:** The act of placing two planets at 60 degrees from each other. It is a sign of cooperation, synergy, and fulfillment.

**Trine:** The act of placing three planets at 120 degrees to each other. It is an easy situation with harmonious energy.

**Aspect:** This is the mathematical term for "relationship" in astrology. For example, one planet is the ruler of another. The first planet in a sign rules another planet.

**Elemental:** Each planet rules an element.

**Cardinal:** Each planet rules a natural action step or direction, such as "create" or "lead." The four cardinal signs are Aries, Cancer, Libra, and Capricorn.

**Fixed:** Each planet rules a fixed principle, such as security and stability or transformation and change. The four fixed signs are Taurus, Leo, Scorpio, and Aquarius.

**Mutable:** Each planet rules changeable qualities such as variety, flexibility, or adaptability. The four mutable signs are Gemini, Virgo, Sagittarius, and Pisces.

**Moon Sign:** This is where the Moon is at in the particular time when you were born. This sign is usually the 2nd cusp of a house in your chart.

**Node:** These are two points, sometimes referred to as "planets", on the orbit of the Moon that sometimes appears to be planets. They indicate unique turning points and are "theme points" in life.

**Houses:** represent the areas of life or activity that each planet oversees. These are known as "houses" of life. There are 12 houses in a birth chart on the zodiac wheel; each planet rules 1 of them.

- **The first house** is the house of self and your central needs.

- **The second house** is communicating with others and social activities.

- **The third house** deals with tools and creative work.

- **The fourth house** is home and family.

- **The fifth house** is romance and pleasure.

- **The sixth house** is your highest learning and inner growth.

- **The seventh house** is about business, partnerships, and friendships.

- **The eighth house** is about bad luck and wealth.

- **The ninth house** is about your outer life.

- **The tenth house** is about your career and your public position in the world.

- **The eleventh house** is about healing and the spiritual path.

- **The twelfth house** is where time comes to an end. It governs the end of the person's life.

**Midheaven:** This is the point at which the chart's Midheaven sign is made. It is the point in the chart that rises over the horizon.

**The South Node:** This is where the Moon is furthest from the Sun on its cycle. It is also called the "Fate Line".

**Descendant:** This is the furthest sign from the Ascendant. Planets in the Descendant sign often represent the direction from the person's life's focus, represented by your Ascendant.

**Astrology:** This is the study of planets, signs, aspects, houses, and other planetary combinations, based on your birth time, date, and place, and their interrelationships. This study is also known as "the science of the stars."

**Birth Time:** This is the time that you are born. This detail may be recorded as 12:00 AM, 12:00 PM, 7:00 PM, and so on.

**Signs:** Signs are 30-degree divisions of a zodiac wheel. Each sign has an individual quality. The twelve signs represent entire areas of life energy.

**Transits:** These are when planets meet in your birth chart. They represent what other people are doing to you, what you are doing to them, or what you are doing to yourself.

**Stellium:** This is when several planets are clustered closely together. It indicates a powerful grouping.

**Zodiac Wheel:** This circle is divided into 12 equal signs. It is also known as the "circle of destiny" or the "wheel of the signs". It is a circle because there are 12 360-degree increments on the wheel on which the planets are judged to be in a sign.

**Chiron:** This is a comet-like object representing the wounded healer or the one needing healing.

**Retrograde:** This is the planet being still and backward. This can affect a chart reading and the world's energy during the event.

**Horoscope:** A written or spoken horoscope forecasts what will happen in the future. It is written in either prose or poetry or in a close paraphrase form.

# 59 Positive Affirmations for Body Astrology

Positive affirmations express the belief that a certain thing is possible. They can benefit anyone striving for a goal by teaching them to think positively. Some people read positive affirmations every day to achieve specific goals. You can benefit by repeating these simple statements to yourself to help you overcome negativity and succeed at your goals.

Repeating positive affirmations help you reach any goal you strive for by increasing your self-confidence, building a positive attitude, and boosting your determination. This helps you visualize your goal and realize the importance of reaching it. This can be any goal you have on your mind!

Affirmations can help you reach your goals faster as they are positive thinking. They involve repeating a phrase or statement until it becomes "second nature."

Now relax and calm down as you repeat each affirmation five times in a row for 2 minutes each. You will listen to the affirmation, and there will be a pause of 2 minutes after each affirmation to give you enough time to repeat the affirmation and let your brain process it.

# 59 Affirmations for Body Astrology

1. My zodiac signs balance me.
2. I am aware of my astrological power.
3. I am an individual; therefore, I am responsible for my happiness.
4. I have good intuition, and my inner strength is profound.
5. I attract my "good one".
6. I am a proactive person.
7. I look and take pleasure in the world that I inhabit.
8. I look where ordinary people do not see anything.
9. I see what's important, and I act from that understanding.
10. I am more than happy when I successfully manage my energy.
11. I am in control of my cosmic powers.
12. I am aware of the natural strength that helps me win, achieve and reach my goals in life.
13. I love to live my life full, inspired, and ever-beautiful.
14. I am a young and beautiful woman who lives with passion and goodwill.
15. I am my Astrologer, Peacemaker, and a Master Healer.
16. My enthusiasm is my strength. I am sensitive, kind, modest, and humble.
17. I give others space and respect their individuality.
18. I am sure to enjoy my life with my handsome Aries man!
19. I am a very charming and attractive person with a warm heart, strong will, and a positive attitude to life.
20. I have a good sense of humor and a soft spot for animals.
21. I have a great passion for nature, music, and painting.
22. I am a responsible person.
23. I am a very energetic and joyful person.
24. I am keen on sports and an active lifestyle.
25. I am a kind and generous person who enjoys life in all dimensions: romance, traveling, and dining out.

26. My dream is to establish a family, provide a stable environment for my loved ones, and share all their love and joy.
27. I am a sensitive and caring person who loves home and family.
28. I am very open-minded and love to share my positive view of the world with others.
29. I am a problem solver and goal-getter by nature who like to meet my goals successfully.
30. I am a very energetic, positive, and hardworking person.
31. I like challenging myself.
32. I am a loyal and faithful person.
33. I am a very active person who is always on the move.
34. I am a nature lover who prefers the comfort and warmth of home to living an adventurous life full of creativity and self-expression.
35. I am in tune with my cosmic energy to guide me.
36. I am motivated and self-assured to achieve my goals in life and find my soul mate.
37. I seek the best in life for myself and my loved ones.
38. I am a kind-hearted person who is trustworthy and very affectionate.
39. I love home and comfort.
40. I get around easily.
41. I am sociable.
42. I am highly motivated.
43. I am a very open-minded person.
44. I dedicate my life to hard work and reaching my goals successfully.
45. I notice that what I value in life is associated with what and whom I surround myself with.
46. My strength is honesty and integrity, guiding my thoughts, words, and actions.
47. The forces of the elements rule my zodiac sign.

48. I cannot describe my zodiac sign in a few words because I use it mindfully and balanced in all life situations.
49. My zodiac sign is ruled by cosmic energy, and the qualities of my zodiac sign make me passionate, consistent, and persistent in life.
50. I love being practical.
51. I am a very creative person full of ideas and plans.
52. I believe in practical solutions to problems in life.
53. I am a friendly person who likes communication.
54. I love nature.
55. I love to be close to my beloved ones and dive into family happiness.
56. I am easygoing and kind, with no time for drama or negativity.
57. I love sharing my passions with others, cheering them up, and being surrounded by feel-good energy.
58. I am full of energy, optimism, and passion.
59. I'm always raising my energy to the level of being positive.

# FREEBIES

## AND

## RELATED PRODUCTS

**WORKBOOKS**
**AUDIOBOOKS**
**FREE BOOKS**
**REVIEW COPIES**

## HERE

**HTTPS://SMARTPA.GE/MELISSAGOMES**

# Freebies!

I have a **special treat for you**! You can access exclusive bonuses I created specifically for my readers at the following link! The link will redirect you to a webpage containing all my books and bonuses for each book. Just select the book you have purchased and check the bonuses!

>> https://smartpa.ge/MelissaGomes<<

OR scan the QR Code with your phone's camera

## Bonus 1: Free Workbook - Value 12.95$

This **workbook** will guide you with **specific questions** and give you all the space you need to write down the answers. Taking time for **self-reflection** is extremely valuable, especially when looking to develop new skills and **learn** new concepts. I highly suggest you *grab this complimentary workbook for yourself*, as it will help you gain clarity on your goals. Some authors like to sell the workbook, but I think giving it away for free is the perfect way to say **"thank you" to my readers**.

## Bonus 2: Free Book - Value 12.95$

Grab a **free short book** with **22+ Techniques for Meditation**. The book will introduce you to a range of meditation practices you can use to help you develop your inner awareness, inner calm, and overall sense of well-being. You will also learn how to begin a meditation practice that works for you regardless of your schedule. These meditation techniques work for everyone, regardless of age or fitness level. Check it out at the link below!

## Bonus 3: Free audiobook - Value 14.95$

If you love listening to audiobooks on the go or would enjoy a narration as you read along, I have great news for you. You can download the audiobook version of *my books* for **FREE** just by signing up for a FREE trial! You can find the audio versions of my books (depending on availability) at the following link.

## Join my Review Team!

Are you an avid reader looking to have more insights into spirituality? Do you want to get free books in exchange for an honest review? You can do so by joining my Review Team! You will get priority access to my books before they are released. You only need to follow me on Booksprout, and you will get notified every time a new Review Copy is available for my latest release!

# For all the Freebies, visit the following link:

>> https://smartpa.ge/MelissaGomes<<

OR scan the QR Code with your phone's camera

# I'm here because of you

When you're supporting an independent author,
you're supporting a dream. Please leave
an honest review by scanning
the QR code below and clicking on the "Leave a Review" Button.

https://smartpa.ge/MelissaGomes

Printed in Great Britain
by Amazon

12421108R00078